Cover illustration by Debra Lumpkins

Cartoons courtesy of Melinda Ellis
Kitetoon Original

Precision maneuvers reproduced with permission of the
American Kitefliers Association
International Sport Kite Competition Rules, Fourth Edition

Sport Kite Consultants
Susan Batdorff
Bob Hanson
Abel Ortega
Peter Werba

SPORT KITE MAGIC!

ADVANCED FLYING TECHNIQUES
FOR MORE KITING FUN

writing and illustrations by David Gomberg

cover illustration: Debra Lumpkins
cartoons: Melinda Ellis

GOMBERG KITE PRODUCTIONS, INTL.
P.O. BOX 113
NEOTSU, OREGON 97364 USA

Table of Contents

Preface

It must be magic. How else can you explain the gravity-defying antics of a modern sport kite in the hands of a skilled practitioner?

Of course, what is magic, but slight of hand, illusion and practice? You don't need special powers to do these tricks, only a bit of special instruction. So think of this book as your magician's manual.

Much of this information is related to competition, but that doesn't mean we expect you to go out and compete. Far from it. The greatest joys of kiting are the simple thrill of flying, the satisfaction of accomplishing something new, or the rewards of flying with or entertaining your friends. If you are ready to move beyond "fun" flying and into high performance, we're here to help.

Our first book, *Stunt Kites!*, was intended as a beginner's manual. "*Magic*" is for fliers who want to push their kite - and themselves - a little further.

In the pages that follow, we'll walk you through a series of advanced flying techniques, a variety of precision moves, and a collection of great tricks. We'll talk about how to tune your kite for high performance. And then just for fun, we'll show you how to fly to music or even indoors with no wind at all.

A large portion of our text is dedicated to specific precision maneuvers. Again, you can use these moves to compete, or just to extend your flying skills. Review the instructions for each figure before you fly it.

The three precision chapters weren't designed for recreational reading, but rather as practice guides. Don't try to read the figures one after another or they may put you to sleep. But even without these sections, we think we've provided a lot of good information and a bit of fun.

Our goal is to promote safe, responsible flying, and to advance technical expertise. And most important, we want you to enjoy yourself.

We hope we've been able to communicate our sense of exhilaration and wonder at what sport kites offer. Sometimes it's hard to explain to people until they try it for themselves. Then, before they know it, they are out there with that uniquely silly grin on their face.

The flying part is just technique. The joy of it all - now that's the _real_ magic.

You've been there so you know what we mean.

Good Winds!

David Gomberg
April, 1996

Introduction - Basic Magic: A Flying Refresher Course

Sport kites can do things no other kite can do.

In the hands of a skilled flier, your kite can amaze onlookers as it loops, dives, and dances its way across the sky under complete control.

With a little information and a bit of practice, you can be that skilled flier. But before you can run, you need to learn to walk. So before we begin to talk about maneuvers, advanced performance control, and fancy tricks, we need to make sure you can launch, fly, and turn.

If you consider yourself a fairly proficient flier, go ahead and skip this "refresher course". On the other hand, if you are just getting started, take the time to master basic control before you move on.

At worst, you'll spend a few extra hours having fun with your kite, and there's certainly nothing wrong with that.

Layout and Launching: For beginners, your flying line should be between 100 and 125 feet long. Shorter lines reduce response time and make the kite move too fast for most inexperienced fliers. Longer lines make maneuvers harder to complete. After you unroll the lines, make sure they're the same length and that they're securely fastened to your handles and kite.

Your kite and all of your line should be laid out before you launch. Look around to make sure that there are no obstacles or people <u>anywhere within reach</u> of your lines. This is the only way to know that you are clear and safe.

Anchor or "stake" your handles down, then walk back to the kite and stand it up using the flylines as a tension against the wind. Be sure the kite isn't standing straight up when you're done. Unless it leans away from the handles a little, it will try to take off and fly by itself!

Go back to the handles and carefully pick them up, keeping equal tension on both lines. Try not to let the kite move. Before you lift-off, complete the "Pre-launch Checklist". Do <u>everything</u> on this list before every launch.

Pre-launch Checklist:

1. Check the area under where your kite will be flying for possible hazards - especially people.
2. Look behind you to make sure you have a clear path if you need to back up.
3. Make sure your flylines have equal tension so that the kite will launch straight.
4. Check the sky for other fliers.

Now, pull your hands straight back down to your sides. The kite should lift right up into the air.

In lighter breezes, combine these arm movements with several smooth steps back. This will add the extra power you need to lift-off cleanly. Later, we will talk a lot more about combining hand and foot movements for better flying.

It's not unusual for new fliers to crash a few times when they first practice launching. That's fine -- as long as you don't hit anyone on the way down.

Safety and Courtesy: Even before you leave the ground, you should be thinking about safety. A maneuverable kite is a PROJECTILE -- capable of doing injury and property damage. Even in a moderate wind, a typical stunt kite can be moving at over 60 miles per hour. If someone gets hit by <u>anything</u> moving that fast, it's going to hurt. So when you fly, remember to fly carefully.

Steering: There are three, and only three, basic steering movements. Any maneuver you do, from simple to the most complex, will just be a combination of Left Turns, Right Turns, and Straight Lines. That's all there is to it!

Later we will learn about several different ways to complete these turns and get slightly different performance results. For now, focus on what we call "pull-turns".

PULL-LEFT
TO TURN LEFT

HOLD EVEN
TO GO STRAIGHT

PULL-RIGHT
TO TURN RIGHT

Remember that "straight" can mean flying straight in any direction, not just up.

Keep turning to the right and you will eventually complete a loop. The fact that the lines have twisted has absolutely no effect on the way the kite flies. Right is still right and left is still left. To get rid of the twists -- just turn in the other direction.

Pulling back on your handles will make the kite fly <u>faster</u>. Your normal reaction in a crash will be to hold the handles tighter and to pull back on them to try and save the situation. That is <u>exactly</u> the wrong thing to do. You'll just make the kite accelerate and hit the ground <u>harder</u>.

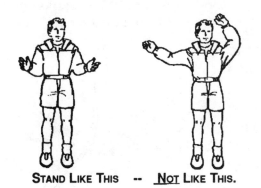

STAND LIKE THIS -- <u>NOT</u> LIKE THIS.

If you think you're going to crash, try moving toward the kite to slow it down. If you need to, <u>run</u> toward it.

While you're flying, keep your arms at your sides. Holding them higher doesn't make the kite go up and holding them farther apart only makes you tire more quickly.

Let the kite do the flying while you just steer.

Later on, we'll be talking about lots of different figures and flying techniques. To improve your skills, practice these three basic maneuvers - the loop, the figure eight, and the square.

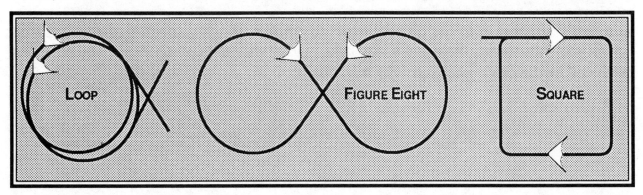

LOOP

FIGURE EIGHT

SQUARE

Landings: A normal, planned landing takes advantage of the fact that, as the kite flies farther "out" to the right or left, it loses drive and speed. Simply fly the kite to the point where it runs out of forward drive at the same time it reaches the ground.

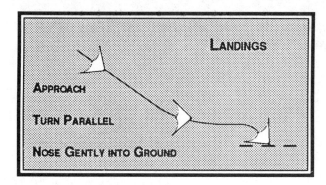

Start at a medium altitude, and steer down toward the ground at the far edge of your flying area. When you reach an altitude of about four feet, turn up slightly so you are parallel to the ground. Then, as the kite slows, make a gentle turn toward the ground. Step forward to ease the kite into a graceful landing.

Picking a Flying Site: Your flying efforts will be much more successful if you find a site with smooth wind and little turbulence. Seek out large open spaces. On a field bounded both upwind and downwind by obstructions, you're better off flying as close as you safely can to the downwind end of the field.

The basic formula for turbulence is that unsteady winds will extend seven times farther than the height of whatever object is causing the disruption. If a tree is 100 feet tall, you need to get 700 feet away to find clean or steady wind.

Tuning: We refer to any adjustments you make to your kite for wind changes or performance as "tuning". Usually, these adjustments are made by moving the place where your flying lines connect to the bridle. This is called the "tow point".

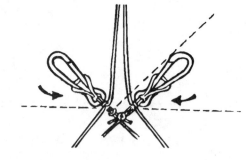

Kites almost always come from the factory with an "average setting" marked on the bridle. Adjust your tow point to these marks and the kite should perform fine in most wind conditions.

The important thing to remember is that the tow points should be even on both sides of the kite. If one tow point is above the mark, and the other is below it, your kite will perform in unexpected ways.

The same is true of your flying lines. They should be exactly equal in length. If the lines are unequal, the kite will think you are pulling on the shorter line and try to turn in that direction.

And that's all there is to the basics! Now, go practice. When you can confidently launch, control your introductory maneuvers, and land, you're ready to move on. So far you have only scratched the surface. Get ready for the fun stuff!!

Chapter 1: A Magical Repertoire:
The Techniques of High Performance Flying

If you are a good sport kite flier, we can help you be a better one.

There are certain basic skills that are used in all types of flying. Whether you are interested in competition, impressing your friends, learning a few tricks, or just feeling a bit more confident with that new high performance kite, practicing these techniques will help.

Before we start, there is one main point we need to emphasize. This is not a sport where brute strength wins. Pulling hard doesn't make the kite fly better. You can be vigorous. You can be extreme. You can be snappy. But don't be forceful. Fly with your head.

The best flying techniques are finesse, precision, and delicacy of control.

There are two kinds of flying - playing and practicing.

When you are playing, you do what you already know how to do. You stay within your limits and usually don't try anything new. You just go out there, take your mind off whatever may be bothering you, and... well... play! Practicing, on the other hand, takes concentration and effort. When you practice, you're focused on improving your skills. You try new things and work at doing old things better. You extend your limits, so that next time, you'll be able to play better.

Throughout this Chapter, we will introduce you to "Practice Assignments". Think of them as sport kite homework. Go out to the field and try them. Concentrate. Fly these assignments over and over until they become a regular part of your flying arsenal.

Then go play some more.

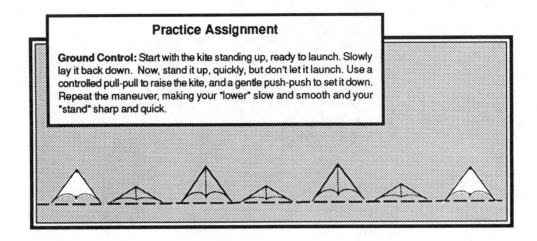

Technique #1: Leading Edge Launch

The Leading Edge Launch is actually a fairly advanced maneuver. But it is one you should learn early.

When you go out to the field, you want to spend your time flying, not walking back and forth from the handles to the kite to set up again after a landing or a crash. But how do you avoid this hundred foot "walk of shame". Easy. Learn to recover and relaunch no matter where or how your kite has landed.

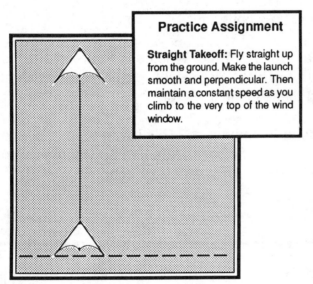

In a normal launch, the base or bottom of the kite is on the ground, perfectly positioned, perpendicular to the flying lines and to you. You just pull back evenly on both lines to launch.

If you have staked out your handles, the kite can be left standing with tension on the lines and the nose leaning back in the wind ready to take off.

And even if you haven't staked the handles down, a gentle, steady pull on the lines will stand the kite up as the standouts and then wingtips make contact with the ground.

But not every situation is perfect.

If your kite has come down unexpectedly, the chances are that it has nosed into the ground. That's good. It's good because you can learn to relaunch, nose down, from almost anywhere in the wind window . And with a bit of practice, you can even make it look like you planned the whole thing.

The key to a leading edge launch is to lean the exposed wing slightly forward, so that enough wind can get under the kite to lift it back into the air.

2

The kite should be toward the edge of the wind with its nose pointing toward the "outside" of your flying area - or away from the center. One wing should be on the ground and the other pointing toward the sky.

Gently draw back on the upper line so that the wing which is not on the ground begins to lean toward you. At the same time, it is important to keep some tension on the lower or ground line.

Don't pull too hard - or the kite will "waddle" over onto the other wing and point back toward the center.

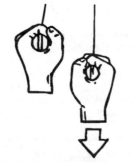

PULL BACK <u>GENTLY</u> ON THE UPPER LINE TO LEAN FORWARD

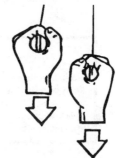

THEN PULL BACK <u>SHARPLY</u> ON BOTH LINES

Pull gently, and just hard enough for the wind to get under the wing and the kite. When the kite is leaning about thirty degrees, pull back sharply on both lines. At the same time, take a few quick steps backwards. This backwards motion will increase the force of the wind on the sail and sustain that increased pressure longer than your arm motions would have.

The nose should swing around into the air, and the kite should lift off. Congratulations!

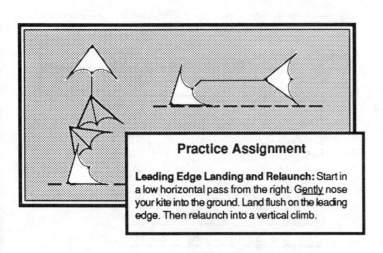

Practice Assignment

Leading Edge Landing and Relaunch: Start in a low horizontal pass from the right. <u>Gently</u> nose your kite into the ground. Land flush on the leading edge. Then relaunch into a vertical climb.

If the kite has landed with the nose pointing toward the wind's center, just tug on the upper line and "flop" it back the other way.

If the kite is too close to the center of the wind, you may need to walk left or right to create a better launch angle.

And please note that "waddle" and "flop" are not technical terms.

At first, you may find the wingtip dragging as you work to turn the kite back into the wind. But with practice, you'll find just the right touch and be able to flip the kite skyward with no problems or unintended ground-touches. So practice!

Leading edge launches are easier if you move the tow point on your bridle slightly toward the nose of the kite. Tune as if you were preparing for slightly lighter wind.

Bridle adjustments make a <u>big</u> difference in how your kite flies. When wind conditions change or you want the kite to respond differently, adjust the tow points. And remember to experiment with your settings whenever you try something new.

Get good enough with this recovery that you can do it anywhere downwind. Then your next challenge will be to perfect the relaunch by balancing the kite on its nose and then flipping it into the wind without touching a wing to the ground at all.

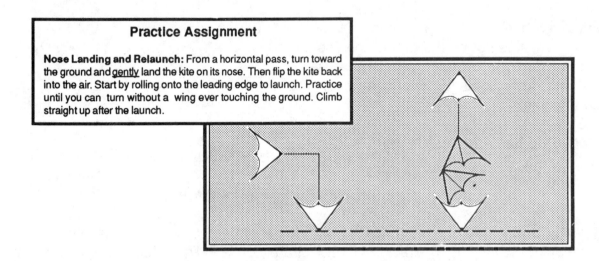

Practice Assignment

Nose Landing and Relaunch: From a horizontal pass, turn toward the ground and <u>gently</u> land the kite on its nose. Then flip the kite back into the air. Start by rolling onto the leading edge to launch. Practice until you can turn without a wing ever touching the ground. Climb straight up after the launch.

Once you perfect the Leading Edge Launch, about the only time you'll need to actually go to the kite is when it is face down with the nose pointing toward you or when the lines have become wrapped or tangled with the kite. And sooner or later, someone will figure out a trick to beat even that.

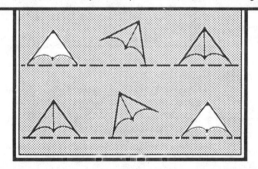

Practice Assignment

Wing Tip Lifts: Start with the kite on the ground. Carefully adjust your line tension to lift and hold the left wingtip up off the ground. Lower the kite, smoothly. Now repeat the maneuver on the right side.

Advanced performers like to incorporate landings, ground work, and relaunches into their routines. But the leading edge launch is more than just a performance trick. It's a practical skill that <u>every</u> flier should know. Forget the "walk of shame". In all but the most tangled situations, learn to get your kite back into the wind using your handles, not your feet.

Technique #2: Straight Flight

There is a big difference between flying fairly straight, and flying <u>really</u> straight. That difference translates into points if you are a competitor, and into personal satisfaction if you are not. Besides, if you want to go anywhere with your sport kite, the quickest way to get there is a straight line.

Now before we begin, there are two things we are presuming about your equipment. The first is that your kite is properly tuned for the conditions and properly balanced as well. You haven't done anything foolish like replaced a broken graphite spar with a heavier fiberglass one. That might make it a little hard to fly straight...

The other thing we presume is that your flying lines are exactly equal in length and that they have been pre-stretched so that one doesn't "give" more than the other in flight.

The secret to flying straight as a ruler is really no secret at all. If the kite and lines are set up properly, then all you need to do is keep your hands locked in place. Don't steer once you have established your line. Your equipment will do the rest.

In practicing controlled straight flight, you have three goals.

First, you want to be able to fly vertically. This means straight up, and straight down. By now, you should be good enough that flying directly toward the ground doesn't intimidate you.

Your second goal is to perfect long horizontal passes. Start in the middle of the wind and work your way lower and lower until you are practically dragging a wingtip. And finally, practice flying diagonally across the wind at a forty-five degree angle.

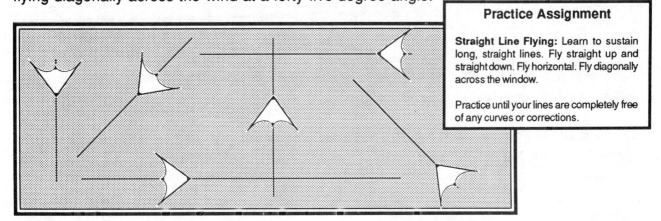

The other thing to remember is that flying straight doesn't mean that your hands will always be exactly even. In fact, about the only time your hands are even is in a vertical line directly in the center of the wind.

When you are flying horizontal, you need to offset the force of gravity. This means maintaining a very slight additional tension on the upper line. If you are flying to the left, you will need to pull back, almost imperceptibly, on the right line.

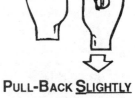

PULL-BACK <u>SLIGHTLY</u> ON THE UPPER LINE IN A HORIZONTAL PASS

When you are flying vertically, you may not necessarily be in the center of the wind. Wind pressure will try to push you toward the center, so you need to compensate by steering slightly the other direction. If you are on the left side of the wind, you may need to steer slightly to the left. And the farther you are from center, the more you will need to adjust.

ROTATE SO YOU FACE YOUR KITE

Finally, no matter what direction you are flying across the sky, remember to turn or rotate your body to keep your hands parallel with your kite lines. If you are facing left, and the kite is to your right, the kite is going to think you are pulling back on one line and will begin to move off that straight line. Facing the kite eliminates this problem.

It's little things like these that make straight lines <u>really</u> straight.

Technique #3: Mastering Turns

Most novice fliers learn to steer by pulling on one flying line. It's basic: pull-right to turn right - pull-left to turn left. When you are ready to straighten out, you push back with the same hand. But the fact is, that pulling on the flyline is only one of the ways you can turn your kite. And the more ways you can make those turns, the more things you can do.

Let's take a look at each of our turning options.

Pull-Push: The "pull turn" is the most natural and basic of turns. As we said before, a pull to turn, and a push with the same hand to recover is the way most fliers learn how to fly.

PULL-RIGHT
TO TURN RIGHT

The pull-push will result in smooth curves and strong, broad maneuvers. Pulling on the line increases power and speeds the kite into the maneuver. Pushing back slows the kite as it recovers. This makes the pull turn useful for curves and circles.

To increase the tightness of the turn, you can push forward with your opposite arm as you pull back on the turning side - much like steering a bicycle.

PUSH-RIGHT
TO RECOVER

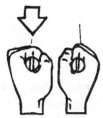

PULL-RIGHT
TO TURN RIGHT

PULL-LEFT
TO RECOVER

Pull-Pull: The pull-pull results in the same, round type of turn as the pull-push. The difference is that you recover by bringing your opposite hand back, even with the turning hand, to finish the maneuver and return to straight flight.

Pull with your right, <u>then</u> pull with your left.

Pulling powers you into the turn. Pulling again powers you out of it. This makes the pull-pull useful for quick curves where you may need that extra power - like hairpins near the ground. You can then return to the normal flying position by bringing both hands in front of you simultaneously.

Remember, when both hands come together, the kite should be flying <u>straight</u> - in whatever direction it happens to be pointed.

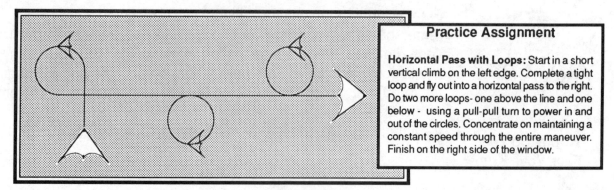

Practice Assignment

Horizontal Pass with Loops: Start in a short vertical climb on the left edge. Complete a tight loop and fly out into a horizontal pass to the right. Do two more loops- one above the line and one below - using a pull-pull turn to power in and out of the circles. Concentrate on maintaining a constant speed through the entire maneuver. Finish on the right side of the window.

Push-Pull: Now let's try something new. If you want to turn to the right, try pushing on the <u>left</u>. Recover by pulling the same hand back in. This may seem a bit unnatural at first, but the results are dramatic corners.

PUSH-LEFT TO TURN RIGHT

Remember that pushing decreases power on one side of the sail. Pulling to recover increases your thrust as you come out of the maneuver.

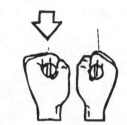

What all this means is that you better start practicing "push turns" if you want to make really sharp corners. This is one of the most useful techniques you can develop. The quickest, sharpest, and most angular turns are created by pushing on one line.

PULL-LEFT TO RECOVER

Think of a "push" turn more like a "punch" turn. Jab your fist out there and pull it back in just as fast. The kite will snap quickly in the opposite direction.

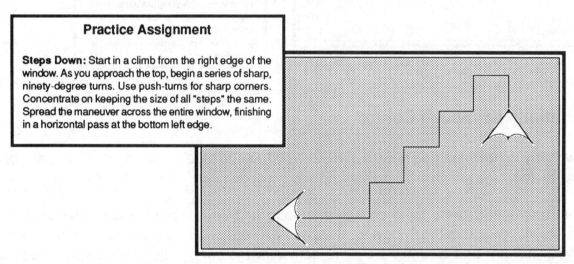

Practice Assignment

Steps Down: Start in a climb from the right edge of the window. As you approach the top, begin a series of sharp, ninety-degree turns. Use push-turns for sharp corners. Concentrate on keeping the size of all "steps" the same. Spread the maneuver across the entire window, finishing in a horizontal pass at the bottom left edge.

Push-Push: So if the push-pull powers you out of a turn, what does a push-push do? It reduces thrust going in, and reduces it even more coming out. Now, why would you want to do that??

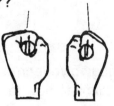

HOLD EVEN TO FLY STRAIGHT

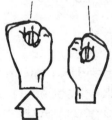

PUSH-LEFT TO TURN RIGHT

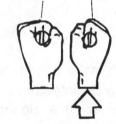

PUSH-RIGHT TO RECOVER

Well, sometimes, you want to slow down your turns. In smaller, tighter maneuvers, the corners may come so quickly that your hands and brain can't keep up. "Dumping" wind out of the sail makes the turns manageable and minimizes oversteering.

Try it. Slower can be better.

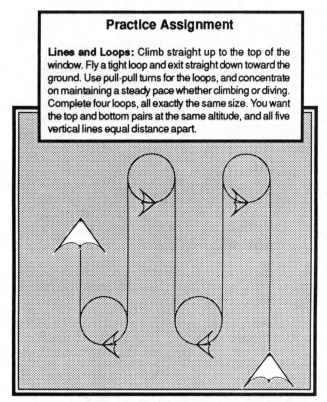

Practice Assignment

Lines and Loops: Climb straight up to the top of the window. Fly a tight loop and exit straight down toward the ground. Use pull-pull turns for the loops, and concentrate on maintaining a steady pace whether climbing or diving. Complete four loops, all exactly the same size. You want the top and bottom pairs at the same altitude, and all five vertical lines equal distance apart.

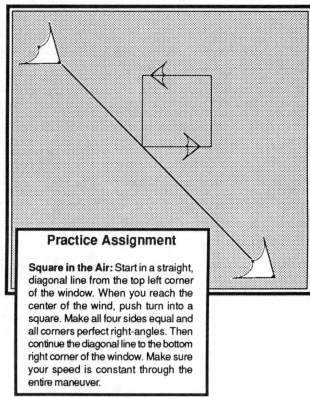

Practice Assignment

Square in the Air: Start in a straight, diagonal line from the top left corner of the window. When you reach the center of the wind, push turn into a square. Make all four sides equal and all corners perfect right-angles. Then continue the diagonal line to the bottom right corner of the window. Make sure your speed is constant through the entire maneuver.

Technique #4: Speed Control

Now that you have learned how to maneuver, you need to learn to control how fast - or slow - you fly, too.

Controlling speed has a lot to do with the grace and beauty of your flight performance. As your kite moves across the flying area, its speed will naturally increase and decrease depending on your altitude and distance from the center of the wind. But precision maneuvers that change pace - that speed up and slow down as they progress - look sloppy and unplanned. And if you're flying to music, you will want to adjust your speed to match the tempo, beat, or mood of your selection, not the force of the wind.

This all means that speed is _very_ important.

You can make limited changes to kite speed by moving your arms. Swinging your arms forward will slow the kite, and pulling them back will speed it up. But there is a limit to how far you can swing your arms. So for real and sustained speed control, use your feet.

Move forward to go slower. Essentially, you are subtracting your own movement from the force of the wind. When you backup, it's the same as increasing the force of the wind.

Save your hand movements for smaller adjustments and quick stops or bursts.

Remember that the strength of the wind changes as you move closer, or farther away from the ground. Friction with the surface causes the wind to slow. In some cases, this change can be as much as five miles per hour, which means that in light wind conditions, the windspeed at low altitudes will be negligible. Lower wind speed translates into slower kite speed.

The effect of the wind on your kite also changes as you approach the edge of the flying window. The kite's angle to the wind changes which results in less pull and slower speed.

What all of this means, is that if you want to fly at a constant speed through the entire vertical and horizontal range of the wind window, you need to do something besides just stand still.

> *Speed control is more than simply a matter of moving forward and backwards. Try moving laterally - or opposite to the direction of your flight. If the kite is moving to the right, side-step to the left. Moving from side to side will not only affect pace in a horizontal pass, it will also increase the distance that you can fly out to the edge of the wind. Later in Chapter 8, we'll even talk about how to force a ground pass completely upwind by moving in the opposite direction.*
>
> *There is a limit to how far you can push and pull with your hands. By using your feet, you change speed in straight lines, or add and subtract power in your turns. The point is to make physical movement part of your performance technique.*

In Chapter 6, we'll talk about tools that can be used to reduce speed in higher winds. These are methods and devices for reducing <u>overall</u> speed. They will slow everything your kite does by one or two miles per hour. When we talk about speed control, what we mean is relative speed - going faster and slower whenever you want.

Remember that steering and speed are two different things. Steering means changing the tension <u>between</u> your two lines, while speed control results from changing the tension on <u>both</u> lines together.

Technique #5: Mid-Air Stalls

Remember the push-push turn? Here is another reason you would want to push on both lines. Draining the wind out of your sails opens up a whole range of tricks and stalling maneuvers. The mid-air stall, or "snap stall" is just the beginning.

Start in a horizontal pass and plan to complete a quick, sharp push-turn up. With both hands close to your body, punch one hand forward, and then just as quickly, pull that hand back in. The kite will jerk, nose up. Now just as your hand is coming back in and the nose of the kite starts to turn, push both hands forward, <u>hard</u>.

These three movements - "punch-pull-double push" - need to be done together quickly.

Practice your timing so you can get the maneuver as quick and crisp as possible. The kite will stop dead in the air.

| PUSH TO TURN VERTICAL | PULL BACK TO STRAIGHTEN | PUSH-PUSH TO STALL |

9

In a lighter breeze, the stall should hold. But if the kite is giving you problems, try one of these "stalling" techniques.

Move your feet. If the kite starts to rise, move forward. If it starts to sink, move back. Remember what you learned about speed control.

If one wing starts to rise, push gently on that line. Pushing will reduce just enough lift to lower the kite back into position.

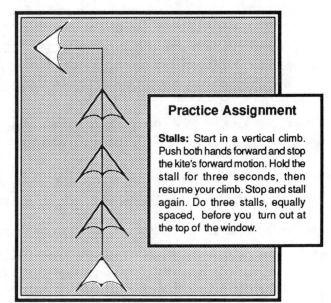

The object of these snap maneuvers is to create turbulence in the air around the kite and in particular, behind it. Smooth air, going over and under the wing, creates lift.

Turbulence interrupts that lift and causes the kite to hang, unstable in the sky. So your goal is to keep air around the kite "disturbed" enough that it doesn't develop enough lift to fly. Then all you need to do is balance it.

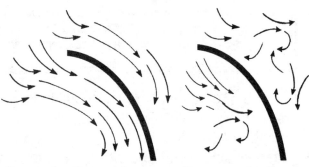

SMOOTH AIR CREATES LIFT   TURBULENT AIR STALLS

A mid-air stall, directly downwind, is a pleasing addition to any routine. And even if no one is watching, it's still a very satisfying trick to perform. Practice holding the stall as long as you can. And then practice popping out by either pulling on both lines to continue the vertical climb, or pulling on one side to turn back into the horizontal pass.

Pulling allows a clean, fast recovery from a stall. Remember, push into a stall, pull out of one.

Stalls will hold more easily if you move the tow point on your bridle slightly toward the base of the kite. Tune as if you were preparing for slightly heavier wind.

Technique #6: Axels

So how would you describe a flat-spin Axel to someone who has never seen one? Easy. You just stop the kite in midair, lay it forward on its face, and then spin it around. Well, at least it <u>sounds</u> easy.

Let's take a look at each of these three elements and see if we can dissect the Axel into something you can easily do.

Stop: You have already learned how to do a stall. Push and Hold. The same stall is a preparatory step for the axel. Just be ready to hold that stall a little longer - and make sure the base of the kite stays parallel to the ground.

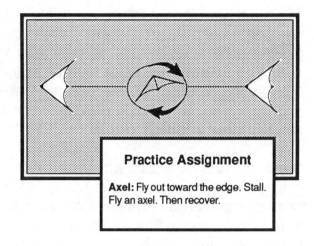

Lay Flat: Next you want to position the stalled kite flat in the sky -- face down -- so the base and nose are almost level. To do this, ease back on one line about six inches. It doesn't matter which line. The point is to ease, not push the line so the kite falls forward into position.

Practice Assignment

Axel: Fly out toward the edge. Stall. Fly an axel. Then recover.

Rotate: This is the tricky part. You want to pull on one line to spin the kite. Make it a short, sharp pull - like a tug or a "pop". This will get one wing moving. At the same time, you need to give the other wing a little slack line so it can follow on around. Remember, pop with one hand and push slack with the other.

Resume: The kite should flat-spin around and then swing nose-up. All you need is to pull on both lines to resume normal flight.

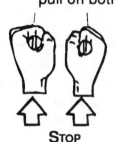
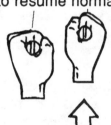
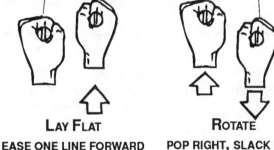
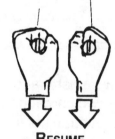

| **STOP** | **LAY FLAT** | **ROTATE** | **RESUME** |
| PUSH AND HOLD | EASE ONE LINE FORWARD | POP RIGHT, SLACK LEFT | PULL ON BOTH LINES |

You are going to have to do all of this lightening fast. Practice the combination of maneuvers in your head before trying them with a kite. Actually move your hands. Push to stall; ease to lay flat; pop and slack to rotate. When you can do it without straining your brain, then try it in the air.

Axels will take practice at first - and just the right touch. But after you get the first, each one you do afterwards will get easier.

Technique #7: Three-Point Landings

Now that you know everything about the basics of advanced flying, you need to spend a little time on an advanced landing. Our goal is to set the kite down gently on its base so it is in position and ready to relaunch.

Approach the extreme left or right edge in a low, horizontal pass. You want to reach your landing zone at an altitude of three feet or less. As you move further and further to the outside, the power of the wind will decrease and the kite will slow. You know you can slow it even more by moving forward.

When you reach the point where you want to land, turn the nose of the kite up, as if you were going to stall. As the kite pivots, push and step forward. The kite should settle backwards into a perfect "Three Point" landing. Keep some tension on the line, and you can relaunch whenever you are ready.

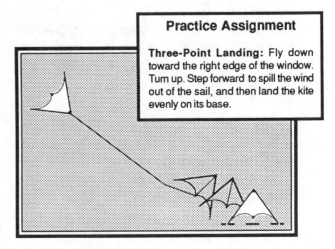

Practice Assignment

Three-Point Landing: Fly down toward the right edge of the window. Turn up. Step forward to spill the wind out of the sail, and then land the kite evenly on its base.

Whenever you land your kite, remember that flylines strung out across the flying field can be a hazard to anyone else in the area. This is particularly true if they are anchored just a few inches off the ground. Be considerate of the people around you, and don't expect them to be familiar with your equipment or your "flying protocol".

Practice the three "C's" of safe kiting: Caution, Courtesy, and Common Sense

Now you are ready for just about anything. You can use your skills to develop fancy routines. You can choreograph your routines to music and fly kite ballet. You can compete or perform demonstrations for your friends. And most important of all, you can fly a little bit better which means you will be safer and have more fun.

Learn each of these techniques and incorporate them into your flying. Practice the assignments we have outlined in this chapter. Later, we will come back and talk about those assignments again.

The skills you have developed will allow some amazing maneuvers. And that's what we are going to talk about next.

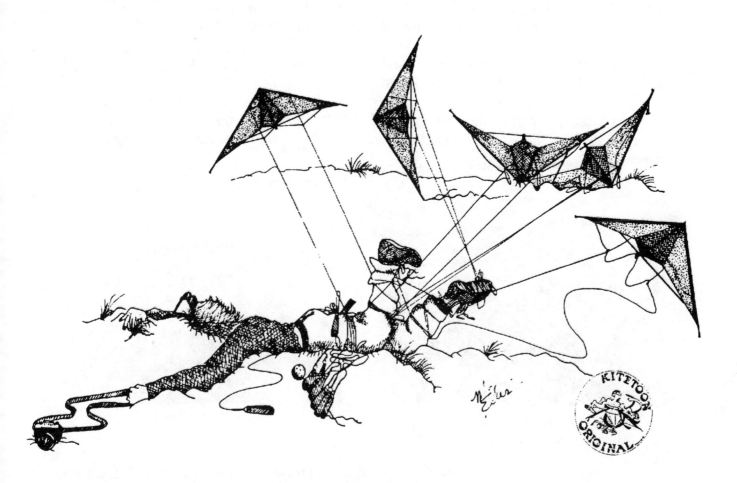

Chapter 2: Setting Up for the Show

Precision flying means that you need to fly - precisely.

Straight lines should be straight, circles round, and squares need even sides with good, sharp corners. It isn't as easy as it sounds, but with practice, it isn't that hard either.

The real test of a precision flier is not just the ability to fly straight lines and crisp angles, but to put them into defined maneuvers. The International Sport Kite Competition Rules (Third Edition) lays out over thirty of these maneuvers for individual fliers. If you choose to explore competition, you will need to know how to fly them. But even if you never go near a panel of judges and their clipboards, mastering precision maneuvers can bring you a great deal of satisfaction.

In upcoming chapters, we'll go through and analyze each of the compulsory figures from the rule book. But first, we need to discuss a few guidelines about precision flying in general and how to read these figures.

The Wind Window

The sky where your kite flies is referred to as the wind "window". In the center of the window is the area we call the "power zone". The kite pulls harder and moves faster. As you move farther from the center and closer to "the edge" of the window, pull and speed decline.

Three things affect the size of the window - the strength of the wind, the efficiency or tuning of your kite, and the length of your flying lines.

In strong winds, the kite will fly over an angle of 120 degrees or more. In lighter winds, that angle shrinks to as little as 45 degrees or less. So in stronger winds, the window will be significantly larger.

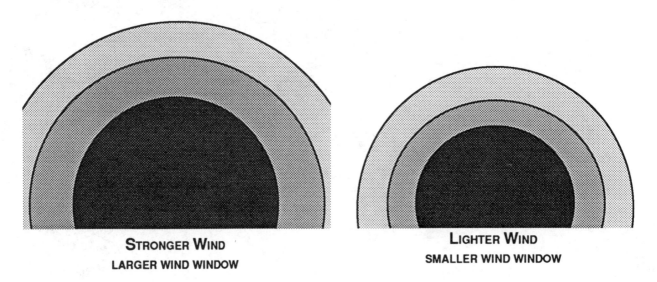

STRONGER WIND
LARGER WIND WINDOW

LIGHTER WIND
SMALLER WIND WINDOW

You can artificially adjust wind speed by physically moving in and out on the field. As we said earlier, you are subtracting or adding your own movement from the force of the wind. Switching to light wind kites, or adjusting your tuning will also allow the kite to push out further to the edge, extending the size of the window.

Another important consideration is the length of your flying lines. By changing the length of your lines, you can offset the effect of wind strength on the window. Shorter lines make the window smaller; longer lines make it larger. Changing from 100 to 150 foot lines will change the size of the wind window by a full one-third.

WITH A LINE LENGTH OF **100** FEET,
 THE WINDOW IS **142** FEET WIDE
 AND **70** FEET TALL.
WITH A LINE LENGTH OF **125** FEET,
 THE WINDOW IS **177** FEET WIDE
 AND **87** FEET TALL.
WITH A LINE LENGTH OF **150** FEET,
 THE WINDOW IS **212** FEET WIDE
 AND **105** FEET TALL.

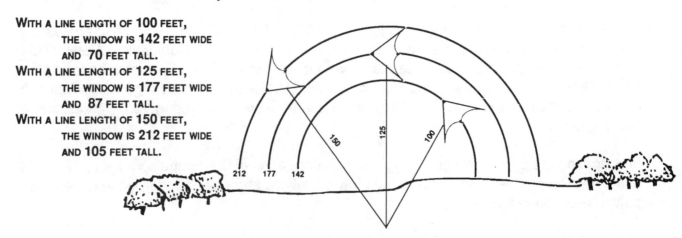

Precision maneuvers are usually easier to complete when flown big and slowly. In smooth winds, longer lines give you more time to prepare for the next turn. On the other hand, if the winds are gusty, long sweeping passes may appear jerky or uneven. Shorter lines will get the maneuver over with more quickly.

No matter what the wind speed, most fliers will try to make maneuvers larger by pushing the kite out to the edge.

Judges and spectators tend to like larger figures, as opposed to smaller ones. This means that longer lines may tend to provide a slight advantage in precision competition. Just remember to keep your line short enough to stay inside the competition field boundaries.

The Maneuver "Grid"

The backdrop for each precision figure is an imaginary grid which is ten units tall and twenty units wide. It is important to remember that these "units" are not necessarily feet or meters. Instead, the grid covers the total wind window, and breaks it into ten percent increments from the center.

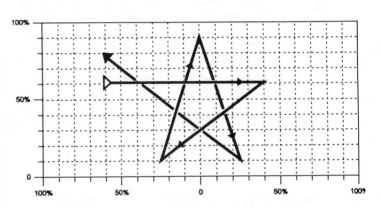

In other words, the grid is as tall and wide as the wind window for each flier, based on wind strength and line length. The diagram shows where in the window each figure starts, the height and width of the figure, and where to finish. **In an average wind, on line of 130 feet, each percentage point on the grid is designed to measure one foot, which means that each ten percent square is ten feet.**

Your goal as a flier, is to duplicate the drawing as perfectly as possible in the sky. Proportions of the figure, as well as direction, count.

Now, the actual sky where you fly is not flat like the grid. As your kite travels across the window from one side to the other, it completes an arc. But the figures are all drawn as if the kite were flying a straight line.

The important thing to remember is that all illustrations are drawn from the flier's perspective. Fly those "straight" lines so they look straight from where you are standing. The judges will hover just behind you to keep the same view.

Some kite designs are better than others for precision flying. The judges are specifically told not to consider the type of kite you are flying when they evaluate your flying. But one thing you should consider is the size of your kite.

Most performance sport kites are seven or more feet wide. In a lighter wind, each square on the figure grid is less than ten feet tall. Since the figures require the <u>spine</u> of your kite to track along the line shown, a wingtip will often be quite close to the ground. This is a dangerous place to be, since you get penalty points for unintentional ground touches - no matter how minor.

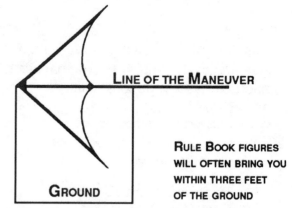

LINE OF THE MANEUVER

GROUND

RULE BOOK FIGURES WILL OFTEN BRING YOU WITHIN THREE FEET OF THE GROUND

To avoid this problem, competition maneuvers are often flown slightly higher than the way figures are drawn in the rule book. Ask the judges about this before you perform, and watch to see what other fliers do.

Depending on the length of your flying line, and the strength of the wind, the window may shrink to the point where it is difficult or even impossible to fly at "ten percent" above the ground. If the center of the kite is at ten percent altitude, the wingtip may well be dragging. And if it isn't dragging, it may well be in danger of snagging any bumps on the ground or taller turfs of grass.

In competition, any ground touch gets you a penalty and a crash gets you a zero. But even when you are flying for fun, a crash or even a touch looks sloppy.

Adjust your figures so the kite won't contact the ground unless you make a real mistake. But don't just change the bottom line. Change the proportions of the whole figure. That way, the maneuver will look the same - but without the crash.

Pace - the Speed of a Maneuver

Whether you are flying up or down, or in and out of the power zone, you're expected to maintain a constant speed throughout the maneuver. We call that speed the "pace" of the maneuver.

Pace is particularly important in precision moves because compulsory figures require you to move across the entire window, diagonally through the power zone, or back and forth in controlled dives and climbs. On gusty days, holding a constant speed may prove nearly impossible, but even in perfect flying conditions, you will need to concentrate on the pace of your maneuver by stepping forward during a dive or backing up during a climb. Fine tuning your flight with hand movements as you progress across the wind window is another important technique to offset changes as you move through the center of the wind.

As we said earlier, precision maneuvers that change pace - that speed up and slow down as they progress - look sloppy and unplanned. To adjust your pace, use your feet! Move forward and back to keep the kite flying at one consistent speed throughout an entire maneuver.

Positioning

The most important thing you can do to get ready for a maneuver, aside from practicing it over and over, is to put yourself in the right place for an effective start. This means you need to properly position the kite for the maneuver, and you also need to position yourself in the field.

Give some thought to how you may need to move during a figure. Are the winds light? Stand downfield so you can step back. Are the winds heavy? Begin at the upwind edge of the field so you have room to move forward. Place yourself so you have room to move. And remember that your kite <u>and</u> your body need to stay inside the marked flying area.

> *Watch the other fliers. See how the wind affects their kite and how they position themselves in the field. Not everyone will make the best choices. You don't have to stand in the same place as everyone else. Learn from their mistakes. And don't be intimidated if the judges are standing in the "wrong" place. Set up where you think is best and let them come to you.*

Once you are in position, take a good look at the wind window where you will be flying. Determine right away where the center, top and edges are. Each of your maneuvers will be based around those parameters. The center is particularly important. As you look at the flying field, draw two imaginary lines dividing it horizontally and vertically. Now fix those imaginary lines in your mind.

Most figures start in a horizontal pass near the top or bottom of the window. Many of the others begin in a vertical dive from the top of the grid, which is most easily reached by turning down from a horizontal pass. Your job is to get the kite to that entry point as smoothly and quickly as possible, and to be able to start the maneuver in a way that will maximize your chances of flying it well.

The best way to position for a horizontal pass is usually to loop back and forth at the outside edges until you are ready to begin.

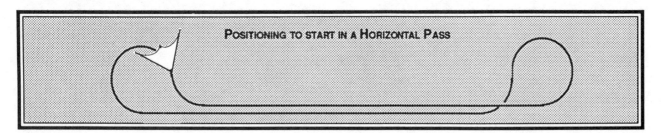

POSITIONING TO START IN A HORIZONTAL PASS

When you are ready to start, turn into your maneuver and call "IN" as loudly as you can. The judges need to know where <u>you</u> think the figure started. As you finish, wait until your kite is exactly where the diagram says the figure ends, and call "OUT".

> *Don't take too much time setting up between maneuvers. Being considerate of the judges is more than good manners. It's good strategy too. A judging "heat" usually lasts over an hour which means that judges get tired. Impatient and bored judges give lower scores. And endless passes by a competitor who isn't ready to start show a lack of confidence.*

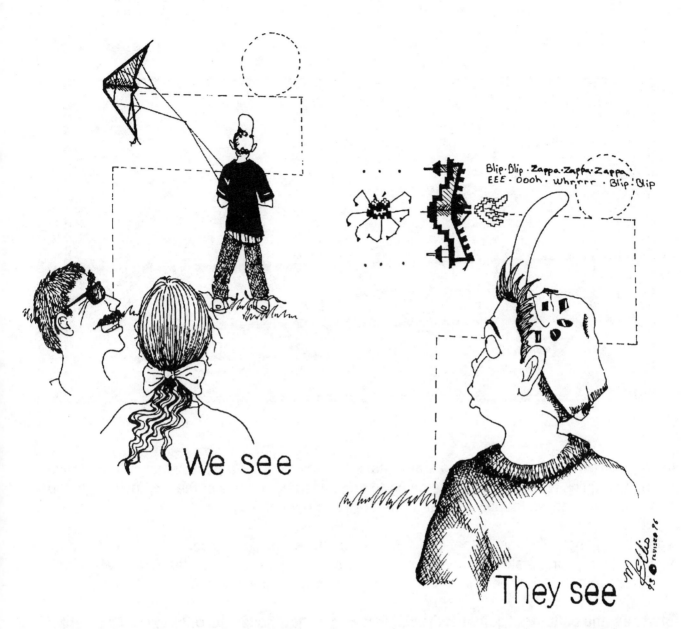

We see

Blip·Blip·Zappa·Zappa·Zappa
EEE·Oooh·Whrrrr·Blip·Blip

They see

Chapter 3: Magic Maneuvers: Flying Introductory Figures

Not every flier is driven to compete. That's fine. But just because you don't want to perform for judges is no reason to avoid rulebook figures.

Flying competition maneuvers is an excellent way to test your skill and improve your ability. The best advice we can give you is to PRACTICE. Study the figures, know the rules, and watch the other fliers for new ideas. Then PRACTICE MORE.

If you're ready for events run "by the rules", your self-confidence, practice, and ability will prepare you for almost any kind of flying you're likely to encounter.

So let's take a look at some of the "official" maneuvers. Start with the easy ones and work your way up. And remember, like we've been saying all along, <u>finesse, precision, and delicacy of control</u> distinguish an expert sport kite flier. That's the secret for getting these figures perfect.

Good Luck!

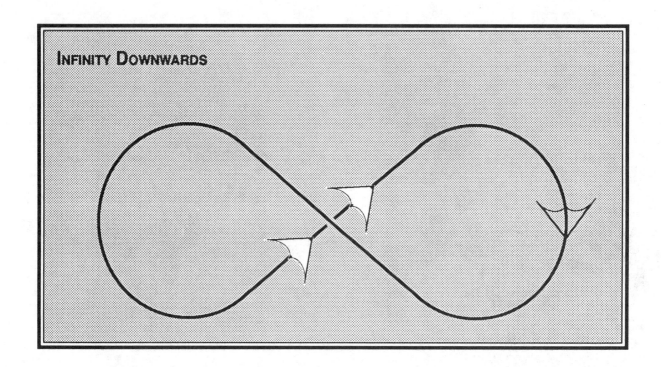

INFINITY DOWNWARDS

Infinity Downwards: X marks the spot - that's the key to flying a good infinity. Three times during this quick maneuver, you are going to cross the same place in the sky just <u>below</u> the center of the window. Identify this target before you begin and fix it in your mind.

The other thing to notice is that this figure is made up of circles connected by diagonal straight lines. Don't make the common mistake of flattening those circles into ovals. Keep them nice and round, especially when you fly around the outside edges.

Start near the bottom left corner of the window. Begin a low horizontal pass toward the center and very close to the ground. Then turn up at a forty-five degree angle directly toward that target in the sky. Just before you reach dead center, call "IN".

Continue flying straight as you climb. Now visualize a perfect circle that nearly fills the right side of the window. As your straight line intersects the circle, begin a smooth pull turn with your right hand. Start to fly that circle you just visualized.

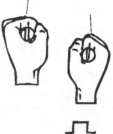

PULL-RIGHT TO CURVE RIGHT

Your speed will vary as you change altitude or move in and out of the power zone. After you go over the top, move forward to decrease speed. As you complete the lower turn and return to diagonal, move back to increase power.

Be careful as you turn under on the right side. Your wing tip will be flying very close to the ground. As you continue curving up, straighten out and fly directly back toward the target point. This will be a long, straight line, so concentrate on avoiding any shaking or "wobbles" in your flight. You may need to move backwards to maintain speed as you climb.

Now begin your second circle. You want it to be a mirror image of the first one. Use a smooth pull turn with your left hand and remember, move forward to decrease speed as you go over the top; move back to increase power as you fly the bottom of the circle.

Again, keep the circle round, and be careful as you turn under on the left. Misjudging the curve could require a sudden correction to avoid ground contact, and sudden corrections are very apparent.

After curving under, straighten out and fly directly back toward the starting point. You are changing from curving to straight flight again. Bring your hands together, and focus on finding that target in the sky. Your objective is to cross the long diagonal in the middle, at exactly the same place as you started. When you get there, call "OUT". And smile!

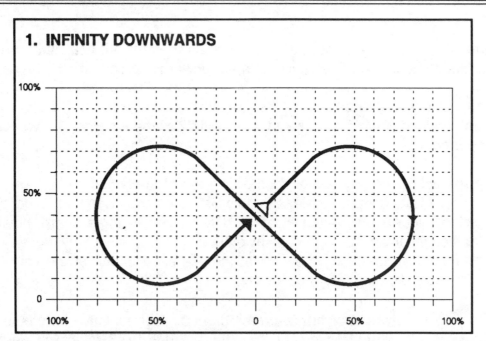

1. INFINITY DOWNWARDS

Competition Spacing: *Circles are sixty-four percent the height of the window. The top is seventy-two percent above the ground, which means that the bottom is at eight percent altitude. Each outside edge is eighty-two percent away from the center of the window.*

Diagonal lines are all perfectly straight. They begin and end thirty-five percent from center and cross in the middle of the window at forty percent altitude. Lines begin ten percent above the ground, and end at sixty-five percent altitude.

IN and OUT should be called at exactly the same location in the sky, directly in the center of the window where the lines bisect each other at forty percent altitude.

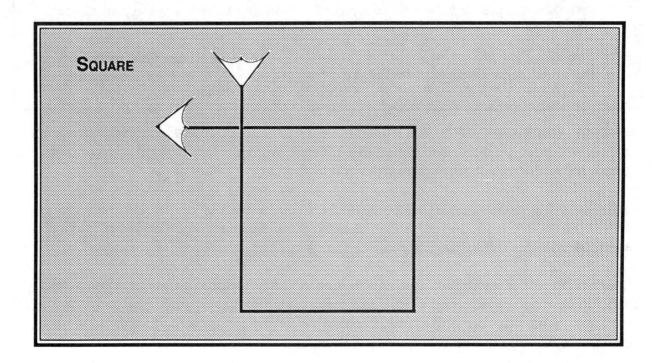

Square: Here is your chance to put those push turns to work. All you need to do is four corners, and four straight lines. Everything is in the power zone so it should be easy.

Notice that two of the lines are equal in length - the ground pass and the vertical climb. Measure them right and your final horizontal pass will cross the first line, the vertical dive, at exactly the right point.

Start high on the right edge. Fly straight across the top of the window and then turn down about one-third left of the centerline. Measure this distance carefully in your mind. If you start in the wrong place, your figure won't be centered in the sky. Flying a sharp, ninety-degree corner to enter the maneuver won't get you any extra points, but will put the judges in the right frame of mind for what's to come. Notice that the maneuver starts at the very top of the window. Call "IN" as soon as you turn down.

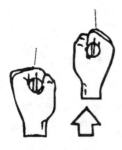

PUNCH-RIGHT FOR LEFT CORNERS

Track straight toward the ground. Your objective here is to minimize any side movement. If you have started on a straight line, perpendicular to the ground, all you need to do is keep your hands even and establish the pace that you want to maintain throughout the maneuver. Since you are in a downwind power-dive, you should move forward to slow your speed.

As you approach the ground, prepare for a crisp, ninety-degree corner. There will be a short delay between when you start the turn, and when it occurs, so start your turn a micro-second early. Punch your right hand forward, then pull it back to complete the turn.

The result you want is a sharp corner that will send the kite back toward the right side of the window with the bottom wingtip just above the ground.

Because of the effects of gravity, your kite may have a tendency to drift toward the ground during a low horizontal pass. Maintain a light "up" pressure by holding your left hand slightly back from the right.

HOLD BACK SLIGHTLY ON THE LEFT TO FLY HORIZONTAL RIGHT

Concentrate on remaining perfectly parallel to the ground. You may need to step back to maintain the same pace that you established on your first dive.

When you have flown nearly one-third the way past center, initiate another left turn by pushing with your right hand. Remember that there will be a delay before the turn, so start early. Move onto a line parallel to the first vertical dive. Climbing is slower than diving, so step back to maintain your pace.

When you have climbed past center, begin your last push turn. If you have measured correctly, the climb will be the same length as the ground pass.

Now all you need to do is fly straight and parallel to the ground as you cross over the path of the first vertical dive. Maintain a slight "up" pressure on your right flying line. That completes the square, but you aren't done yet. Keep flying straight a few feet longer. The figure isn't finished until the diagram says it is finished. When you reach that point, then you can call "OUT" and relax.

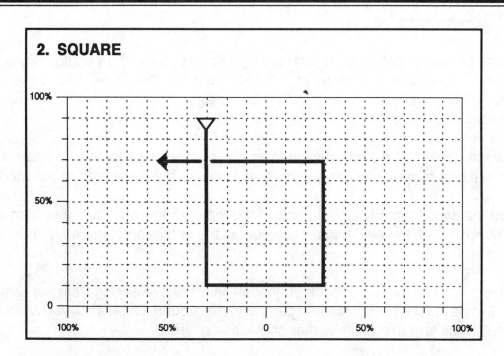

2. SQUARE

Competition Spacing: All vertical lines are thirty percent off center. The square begins in a dive ten percent down from the top of the window. The bottom horizontal line is ten percent off the ground, and the top horizontal is at seventy percent altitude. The figure ends fifty percent left of center.

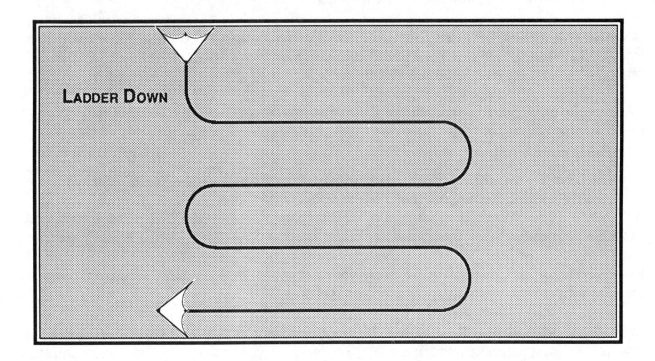

Ladder Down: Careful mental measurements are the key to the Ladder. Divide the sky into four equal slices, then fly the horizontal lines that separate each of them. If your slices are too big, you will run out of space before you reach the ground. If they are smaller than needed, you'll have too much room left over.

Notice that the turns connecting each slice are tight curves rather than angles. Try using the pull-pull technique. Anticipate the turns and don't pull out too soon <u>or</u> too late. Either mistake will throw you off-line and your corrections will be obvious. Your objective is a series of four, perfectly spaced, parallel lines.

Generally, each horizontal pass is designed to be roughly two kite widths apart. But that depends on the size of your kite, the length of your line, and the strength of the wind.

Start high on the right edge. Fly straight across the top of the window and then turn down at the point half way left of the centerline. The figure starts at the top of the window so call "IN" right away.

Begin a curving left turn by pulling back on the left line. Start releasing from the turn <u>before</u> the nose and spine of your kite have come parallel to the ground. Otherwise, you will oversteer and come out of the turn at a much higher angle than planned.

Fly out of your first turn parallel to the ground and headed toward the right side of the window.

Here is an important note: When we talk about turning right, we mean the kite's right. The kite may angle up, go into a loop, or actually fly toward the left side of the window. But <u>right always means the kite's right and left means the kite's left</u>. Don't get confused.

Keep your flight path straight and avoid any shaking or "wobbles". Because of the effects of gravity, your kite may have a tendency to drift toward the ground. Maintain a light "up" pressure by holding your left hand slightly back from the right. Concentrate on remaining perfectly parallel to the ground.

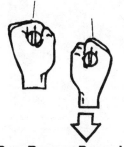

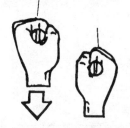

PULL-RIGHT TO POWER IN

When you have crossed the center of the window and flown almost half way across the other side, begin your second turn. Pull-right to turn under. Pull-left to recover and bring your hands even. Pulling powers you into the turn. Pulling again powers you out of it.

Remember to anticipate so you don't oversteer, and move onto a second parallel line. Now all you have to do is repeat the process two more times. Your third turn should occur directly below the position where you originally turned into the maneuver. Your fourth one should be directly under the second.

Focus on proper spacing so you don't run out of room on the fourth and final horizontal pass. Skim along, very close to the ground, and as you pass under the position on the left side of the window where you started the maneuver, call a loud "OUT".

PULL-LEFT TO POWER OUT

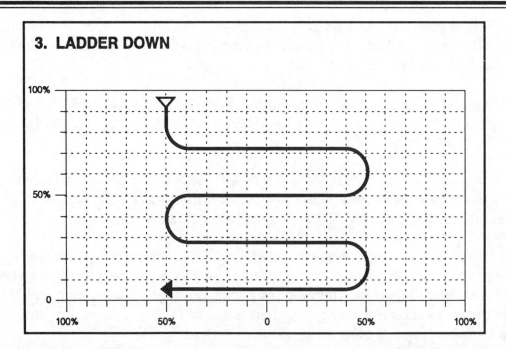

3. LADDER DOWN

Competition Spacing: *IN is called fifty percent left of center at an altitude of ninety percent.*

The first horizontal pass is at an altitude of seventy-one percent. The second pass is at forty-nine percent, the third at twenty-seven and the last very low at five. All horizontal passes cover eighty percent of the window - forty percent on each side of center. Turns are ten percent wide and twenty-two percent high.

OUT is called fifty percent left of center at an altitude of five percent.

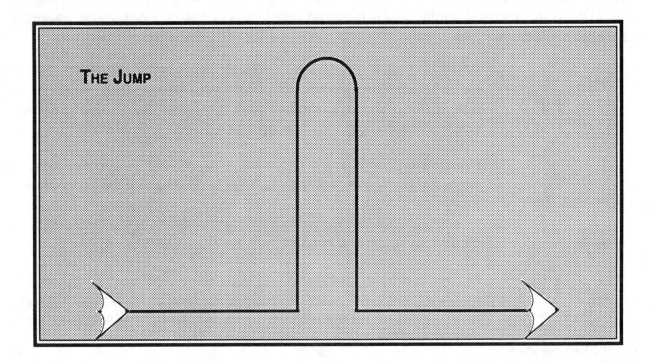

THE JUMP

The Jump: This is your first chance to combine push turns and pull turns in one maneuver. Don't be intimidated by the mixture of styles. After a bit of practice, it will become natural. Just remember, push for angles, pull for curves.

Because of the amount of time spent in low ground passes and straight vertical climbs, you will need to step back a lot during this figure to maintain speed or power. Start deep in the field so you have room to move.

The trick to completing a stylish Jump is to make sure the first and second horizontal passes are on the same line - that is, the same distance off the ground. Be careful, also, not to oversteer on the top curve or you will have to make very visible corrections.

Start with a horizontal pass from the right side flying out to the left edge. This will give you one last chance to check the speed of the kite and put you in the best position to begin the maneuver. Turn under to start the ground pass back to the right. Remember, pull-left to turn under. Pull-right to recover and bring your hands even. Pulling powers you into the turn. Pulling again, powers you out of it.

Make sure you are flying straight and just above the ground. Then call "IN".

Keep your flight path straight and avoid any shaking or "wobbles". Because of the effects of gravity, your kite may have a tendency to drift off line. Concentrate on remaining perfectly parallel to the ground.

Ground passes in lighter wind require additional power. Move back to maintain pace. Then as you approach the center of the window, push with your right to turn sharply up. Your objective is a crisp, ninety-degree corner. Remember that there will be a short delay between when you start the turn, and when it occurs, so start your turn a micro-second early.

Continue to move back through the vertical climb. Maintain the same pace as your horizontal pass and again, try to avoid any drifting. Keep your hands together to fly straight.

PULL-RIGHT TO TURN UP AND OVER

As you approach the top of the window, begin your pull-pull turn to the right. Continue to step back to maintain power and be careful not to oversteer. Start releasing from the turn <u>before</u> the spine of your kite has come perpendicular to the ground. Then, make sure that your vertical dive is exactly parallel to the vertical climb.

Now, finally, you have a chance to move forward and recover a bit of that ground you have been giving up. Slow the kite in the dive to maintain an even pace. As you approach the ground, prepare for another push turn. Time it so you are exactly the same distance from the ground as your first horizontal pass. Push-right to turn the kite left - toward the right side of the window.

PULL-LEFT TO RECOVER TIME YOUR RELEASE CAREFULLY

Continue your straight horizontal flight and as you approach the right edge, call "OUT". Wasn't so hard, was it?

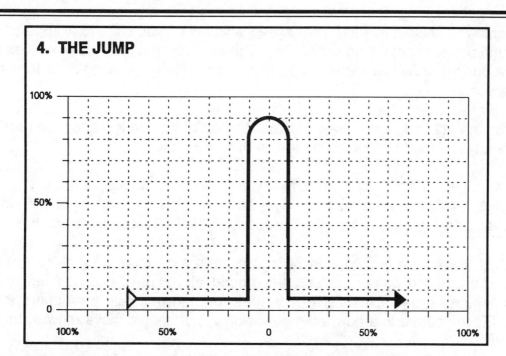

Competition Spacing: IN and OUT are called thirty percent from the outside edges. The horizontal passes are at five percent altitude - <u>very</u> close to the ground.

Vertical turns are ten percent left and right of center. The reverse turn is ten percent high and twenty percent wide. It peaks ten percent from the top of the window.

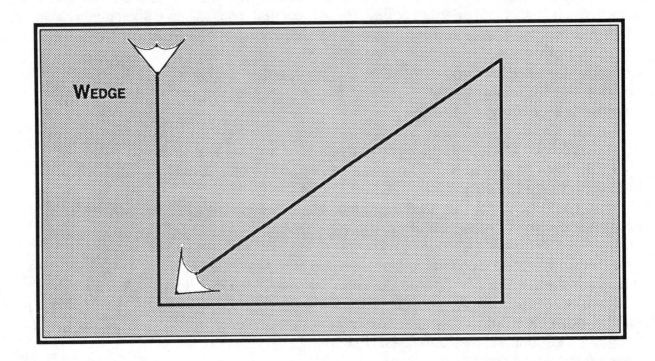

Wedge: Straight lines and sharp angles. By now you know that angles require - that's right - push turns.

Long diagonal lines also mean that your speed will vary as you change altitude or move in and out of the power zone. Diving kites fly faster than climbing ones. As always, keeping the same pace during the whole maneuver is important. Change your position to maintain a constant speed.

Start high on the right edge. Fly straight across the top of the window and then turn down at the point nearly two-thirds left of the centerline of the window.

Impress the judges early. Flying a sharp, ninety-degree corner at this point won't get you any extra points, but will put spectators in the right frame of mind for what's to come. Notice that the maneuver starts at the very top of the window, so call "IN" as soon as you turn down.

Track straight toward the ground, minimizing any side movement or shaking. If you have started on a straight line, perpendicular to the ground, all you need to do is keep your hands even. Concentrate on establishing a pace that you can maintain throughout the entire maneuver. Since you are in a downwind power-dive, you should move forward to slow the kite's speed.

As you approach the ground, prepare yourself for a crisp, ninety-degree corner. Push right to turn the kite left. Anticipate the turn and time it so you make a sharp right angle just one kite width above the ground. Fix the location of this turn in your mind. You are going to need to find this spot again later.

After you turn, concentrate on remaining perfectly parallel to the ground. Keep your flight path straight and maintain a slight "up" pressure to offset the effects of gravity. You may need to step back to maintain the same pace that you established earlier.

When you have flown nearly two-thirds of the way past center, initiate another left turn by pushing with your right hand. Move onto a line parallel to the first vertical dive. Remember that climbing is slower than diving. Step back to maintain your pace.

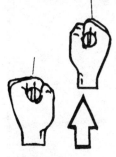

PUSH-RIGHT HARD TO TURN SHARP

Now the tricky part. At the same altitude where you began the maneuver at the top of the window, you need to make a very sharp left turn. Push-right - hard! Pop the nose of the kite around and aim it directly at that corner over on the bottom left side.

It is a long, straight diagonal flight back to the finish line and you need to pass right through the center of power zone. Make any corrections minor so they are less visible and don't let changes in wind pressure throw your cadence off. Move slowly forward and back if you need to adjust the kite's speed.

Keep focused on the point where you made that first corner. When you get there, call "OUT" — and then turn up to avoid crashing.

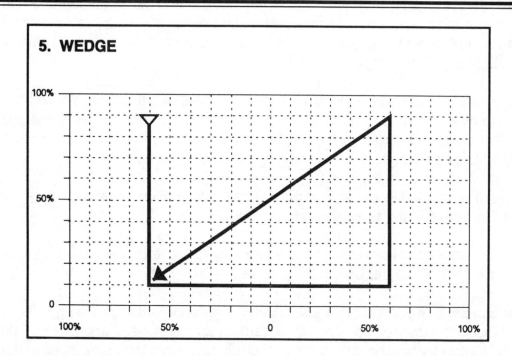

5. WEDGE

Competition Spacing: IN is called sixty percent left of center and ten percent from the top of the window. The bottom line is ten percent off the ground with the second corner sixty percent right of center.

The final turn is ten percent from the top. The turn involves a one-hundred-thirty degree angle which bisects the first corner. OUT is called at ten percent altitude.

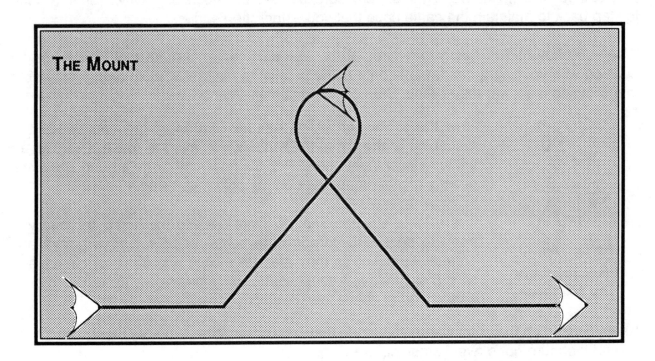

THE MOUNT

The Mount: This is another maneuver where you need to find the exact center of the window and fix it in your mind before you begin. After a short horizontal pass, you will angle up and aim directly at this center target. And your flight path will cross here as you finish a high circle and return to straight line flying.

Obviously the top of this figure is not a full circle, but more of a teardrop. We call it a circle to remind you to make it round, not oval. Don't make the common mistake of flying it too narrow. Also note that the tear is one-third the height of the full figure, even though it doesn't look it. Don't fly too big or too small.

The amount of time spent in low ground passes and diagonal climbs may require you to step back a lot. Start deep in the field so you have room.

Begin in a horizontal pass from the right side flying out to the left edge. Turn under to start the ground pass back to the right. Call "IN" right away.

Make sure you are flying straight and just above the ground. You know that ground passes in lighter wind require additional power. Move back to maintain pace and power, and keep a slight "up" pressure by holding your left hand a little back from the right. By now, you should have horizontal passes down to a science.

Concentrate on remaining perfectly parallel to the ground. Then as you pass the point halfway out from the center line, angle up forty-five degrees. Make this a short push turn with your right hand. As you recover, the nose of your kite should be aimed directly at the center of the window. Return to straight flight.

USE A SHORT PUSH
FOR A 45 DEGREE TURN

Even though you are flying into the power zone, you may need to move back through the diagonal climb to maintain the same pace as your horizontal pass. When you reach the centerpoint, prepare to fly the circle.

Pull-left to make the curve. Then, as you come around, straighten out and aim back toward dead center. Remember to anticipate so you don't oversteer. Start releasing from the turn <u>before</u> the nose of your kite is aiming at your target.

You should now be on a diagonal line back toward a point on the ground, almost halfway right of center. Move forward to reduce speed. Then as you approach the ground, push with your right hand to return to a horizontal pass. Your objective is to position this second horizontal pass exactly the same distance above the ground as the first one. Maintain pace. Fly straight out to the right edge, and call "OUT".

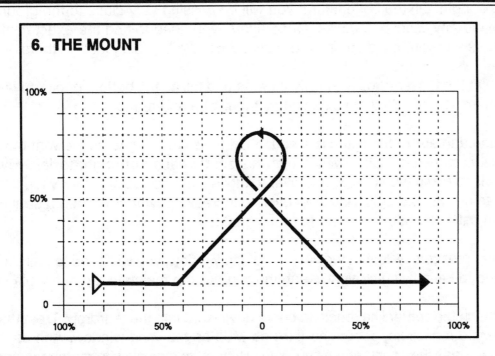

6. THE MOUNT

Competition Spacing: *IN and OUT are called twenty percent from the outside edge on a horizontal line ten percent above the ground. Angle up forty percent left of center.*

Curves for the circle begin and end sixty percent above the ground. The circle is twenty-five percent wide and peaks twenty percent from the top of the window. The second diagonal crosses the first one at a right angle in the center of the window and returns to horizontal flight forty percent right of center.

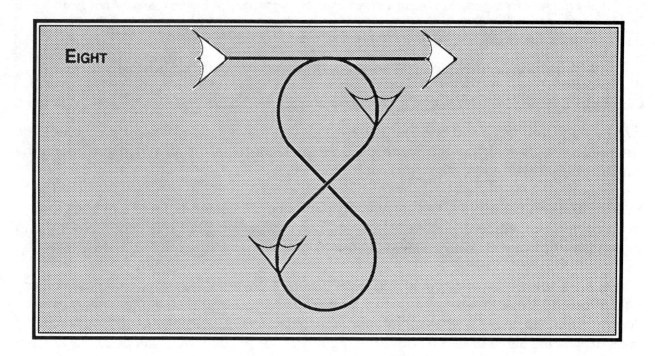

Eight: This is a long narrow maneuver that fills the window from top to bottom, but never flies very far left or right. On the bottom turn, you will be passing very close to the ground, so be careful to avoid any wingtip touches. Once again, you need to find the exact center of the window and fix it in your mind before you begin. Picture a big, diagonal "x" there.

Make sure that the top teardrop is exactly as wide and tall as the bottom one. You might want to think of them as circles if that helps you fly them nice and round.

The beginning and end of the figure is a horizontal pass flown higher in the window than any other precision maneuver. Start with a high horizontal pass from right to left. Fly straight across the window and then turn <u>up</u> and over to move into position at the very top. Use a pull-pull turn, leading with the right, and step back to increase power. Establish a straight line to the right and call "IN" about one-third from the center.

Because wind pressure is light at the very top of the window, you will need to pull slightly with your left hand to keep flying straight. Keep moving back to maintain a reasonable speed.

When you reach the center line, begin to curve downward into the teardrop. Treat the top half as if this were a real circle, about one-third as wide as the wind window. And start moving forward to decrease the speed of the kite. You will need to stay slow to match the pace of the horizontal pass you just finished. Be prepared to adjust speed as you change altitude and move through the power zone.

When you complete the outside arc, straighten out and aim the nose of your kite right at the center of the window. Keep your movements smooth to form curves, not angles. You want to be flying at a forty-five degree diagonal so the first teardrop fills the entire top half of the window.

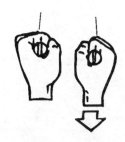

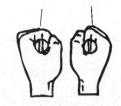

EASE INTO THE TURN FROM THE HORIZONTAL LINE

PULL BACK MORE TO FORM THE CIRCLE

BRING YOUR HANDS EVEN TO FLY STRAIGHT

Now your objective is to complete a second teardrop in the bottom half of the window. Make it a mirror image of the top one, just as tall and just as wide. You can stop moving forward as you finish the dive. This will provide extra power as you fly under at the bottom of the window.

As you finish the bottom teardrop, you will pass through the center of the window again. Remember that imaginary "x"? Keep flying straight and begin to move back if you need extra power or speed during the climb. Finishing the second teardrop should be easy at this point.

As you reach the top of the window, straighten out into a high horizontal pass. Ease into it. Make this pass look like a continuation of the original horizontal line that started the maneuver. Keep moving back to generate the power and lift you need.

When you are a third of the way right of center, call "OUT", catch your breath from all that moving back and forth, and then walk over to a good starting point for your next figure.

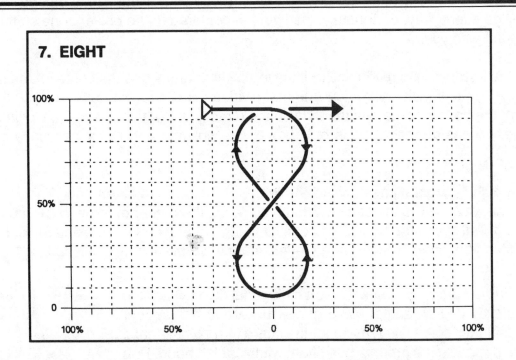

7. EIGHT

Competition Spacing: The top horizontal and bottom curve are at the extreme edges of the window, at ninety-five and five percent respectively. IN and OUT are called on the top horizontal line, one-third out from center. The balance of the figure is thirty-five percent wide with lines crossing at the exact center. Teardrops are each forty-five percent tall.

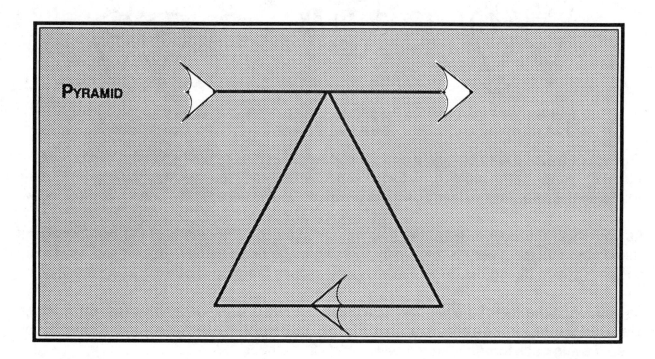

PYRAMID

Pyramid: Ready for lots of sharp angles? Been exercising your left hand? You'll need hard push turns and good measuring skills to put all of these lines where they belong. A bit of practice will go a long way. Fortunately, the figure is centered in the power zone so the wind will be working with you.

The key to the Pyramid is to recognize that the top of the triangle and the center of the bottom horizontal are on an imaginary vertical line that divides the window in half. Another thing to notice is that the bottom corners of the triangle are directly below the IN and OUT points. You can use these kinds of observations to improve your spacing and the appearance of your maneuver.

Start with a high horizontal pass toward the left. Turn under, straighten your flight, and call "IN" about half way back to the center. When you reach the center of the window, push with your left hand. Anticipate the turn so you can hit it <u>right on</u> that imaginary center line. Fix this turning point in your mind. You will need to find it again before you are finished.

If you have turned properly, you will be on a diagonal dive toward the ground at a sixty degree angle. Move gently forward to adjust your speed, but maintain some line tension for the sharp turn coming next. Now, as you approach the ground, push hard with your left hand. Pop it out there! You want to snap the kite around a full one hundred-twenty degrees, parallel to the ground.

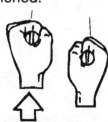

ALL TURNS ARE RIGHT
ANTICIPATE !
PUSH-LEFT TO ANGLE RIGHT
FOR SHARP TURNS PUSH HARD

Move back to maintain pace and power, and keep a slight "up" pressure on the right line to keep your flight parallel to the ground.

As you cross that imaginary line at the center of the window, remind yourself that you are only half finished with the horizontal pass. Turn up too soon or too late, and you'll miss either your angle or the top of the triangle. Fly an equal distance out to the left as you prepare for your next tight angle. Now, push hard with your left hand again. This will be another one hundred-twenty degree turn.

Pivot the kite back sharply around and aim it directly at the top point of the triangle. To maintain a constant speed, you may have to move again. Step back gently as you climb. Pass through the power zone, and then prepare for your last turn.

At exactly the same point where you entered the triangle, snap another push-turn with your left hand for the final horizontal. Your objective is to make it look like a continuation of the original line that started the maneuver. Fly out to the point directly over the bottom right corner of the triangle, and call "OUT".

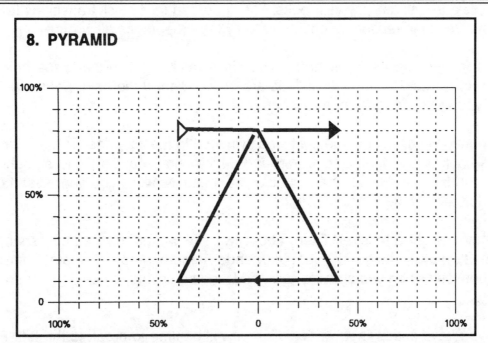

8. PYRAMID

Competition Spacing: IN and OUT are each forty percent from center on a horizontal line twenty percent from the top of the window. The turning point for the top of the triangle is directly in the center.

Outside edges of the triangle are also forty percent from the centerline. The bottom horizontal is at ten percent altitude. Note that all inside angles are sixty degrees. A common error is to fly them at forty-five.

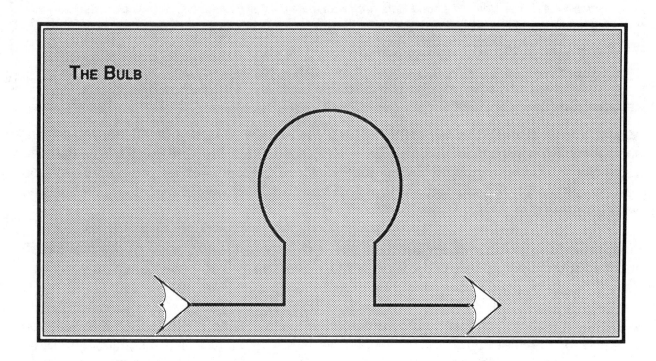

THE BULB

The Bulb: This one isn't as easy as it looks. The figure requires quick transitions from angles to curves, and for some reason, people tend to fly the proportions all wrong.

Visualize the top portion as a full circle. The circle takes up two-thirds the height of the maneuver. In other words, the vertical lines are only one-third the height of the entire Bulb. This means you will need to fly them very quickly.

Start with a horizontal pass from the right side flying out to the left edge. Turn under to start a ground pass back to the right. Set your speed. Make sure you are flying straight and just above the ground. Picture the full maneuver in your mind. Now, as you approach the halfway point on the left side of the window, call "IN".

Continue to fly straight and level. Then, about two kite widths from center, snap a sharp, ninety-degree turn by pushing with your right hand. Remember to anticipate. There will be a short delay between when you start the turn, and when it occurs, so begin to push a microsecond early.

As soon as you have established vertical flight, it will be time to break to the left. Push with your right again, but not as hard as before. Aim for a forty-five degree angle. Your objective is to create a clear angle as you steer into the round part of the figure.

Immediately after pushing right, begin to pull back. You need a quick, smooth transition from a push-turn to a gentle pull-turn. Remember, push for angles, pull for curves. Visualize a perfectly round circle that peaks three-fourths of the way to the top of the window. Maintain a steady pull with your right hand and fly that circle.

To keep the flight lines fluid, and your speed constant, you will need to keep moving throughout the maneuver. Move back as you climb. Move forward as you go over the top. Move forward more as you dive and complete the circle.

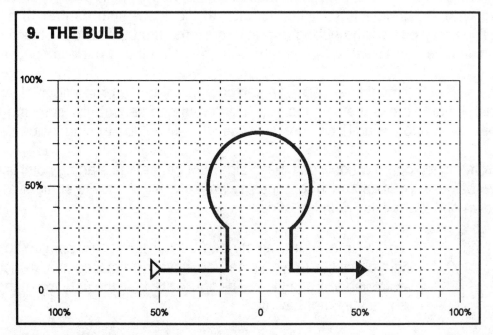

QUICKLY SHIFT FROM CURVES TO ANGLES

PULL- RIGHT TO CURVE

PUSH- RIGHT TO ANGLE

Just as you begin to turn under, at precisely the same altitude as you entered the circle, turn out. Push with your right again. Create another clear angle that shifts the kite onto a vertical line perpendicular with the ground.

Stabilize your flight, and then push hard with your right to form the final turn. This will come very quickly, so prepare yourself. Don't oversteer. You've come too far to mess things up now.

Move back to power yourself out of the turn, but watch your pacing to make sure you're not flying too fast. Then simply fly out, half way to the right edge and call "OUT".

If you aren't convinced the figure was perfect, fly it again. Improvement comes with practice.

9. THE BULB

Competition Spacing: The figure begins at an altitude of ten percent, half way out to the left. Turn into the vertical line fifteen-percent from center. Angle into the circle at thirty percent altitude.

The circle is fifty percent wide and peaks twenty-five percent from the top of the window.

Exit angles mirror those used to enter the figure. OUT is called fifty percent from center on the right at an altitude of ten percent.

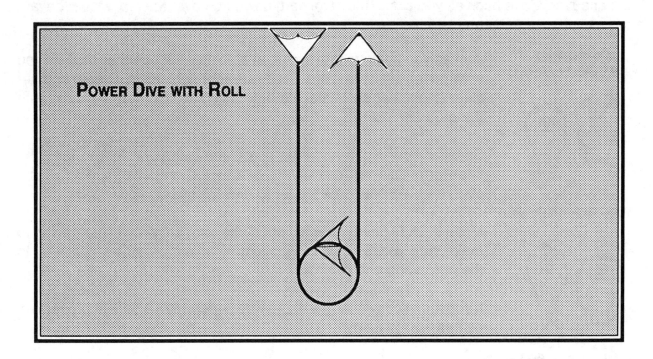

Power Dive with Roll: Here is your first chance to include a spin as part of a precision maneuver. The tricky part will be pulling out at exactly the right time. Your objective is to fly two parallel lines, perpendicular to the ground, with the spin placed perfectly between them.

Consider the size of the maneuver carefully, and compare it to the proportions of your kite. A common mistake is to make the spin too big. Don't overcompensate by spinning too small either. Unless the window is quite compressed, the kite will not be turning inside its wingtip.

Approach from the top of the window on the left side. Notice that the starting point is very high up, so move back on your approach to generate an extra bit of lift. Fly straight across and then turn down about one kite width left of center.

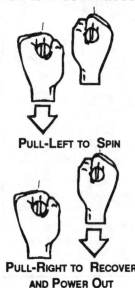

PULL-LEFT TO SPIN

PULL-RIGHT TO RECOVER AND POWER OUT

Try flying a sharp, ninety-degree corner at this point. You will need this precision move since you have no time on the vertical dive to establish a straight line. The figure starts at the very top of the window, so call "IN" right away.

Track straight toward the ground. All you need to do is keep your hands even. Concentrate on establishing a pace that you can maintain throughout the entire maneuver. Since you are in a downwind power-dive, you should move forward to slow the kite's speed.

As you approach the bottom of the window, stop moving forward to tension the flying lines. Then begin your spin by pulling on the left line. If the winds are light, move back to increase power. If the wind is heavier, brace yourself for the extra pull.

Watch out for the ground here. Remember that lines in the illustrations are based on the nose and spine of the kite, not the wingtip. Even brushing the grass will cost you points so time your spin carefully. Don't "skid" out of the turn or let the kite's inertia push you lower than you planned. You want to be close enough to the surface to be exciting, but not so close it is dangerous.

The temptation will be to spin the kite fast so the wind roars off the sail. Don't do it! Timing your exit is crucial, and slower movements allow more precise calculations.

Turn over the top and come back under a second time on the spin. Anticipate your release so the nose of the kite will be aiming straight up. As you approach that point, pull back on the right line to straighten, and move back to increase power for the climb.

Continue to move back through the vertical climb. Maintain the same pace as your vertical dive and again, try to avoid any drifting to either side. Keep your hands together to fly straight.

As you reach the top of the window, call "OUT". You can't go farther because you have run out of flying space. Either stop and hover, or push left or right to exit. Just make sure you call "OUT" before you do something else. Otherwise, the judges will count anything extra you do. And in this case, extra movements don't help.

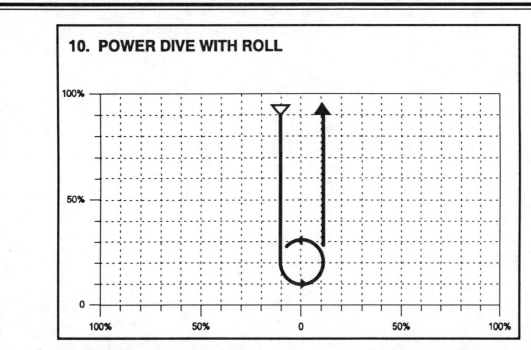

10. POWER DIVE WITH ROLL

Competition Spacing: IN and OUT are at the very top of the window. Vertical lines are ten percent off center. The spin is twenty percent in diameter, and is flown ten percent off the ground.

Chapter 4: Magic and Music: Designing a Kite Ballet

Kite ballet allows you to give your kite a great deal of "personality". When you design a ballet, your challenge is to use music and maneuvers that develop and demonstrate that personality. You can even use you own personality as a model!

Some people think that planning and flying a kite ballet is hard. It isn't. What could be more natural, more fun, more relaxing than flying your favorite kite while listening to your favorite music?

Doing it in public or bringing home trophies - well - that's just an added bonus.

Ballet Basics

To create a good, polished ballet, you need to carefully choose your music, and plan out your routine. Planning is important. You don't want your music to end before you finish your performance. Let's begin our examination of sport kite choreography by looking at the different components of a musical routine.

Musical Selection. It's important to fly to music you like. After all, the first person you need to please is yourself. And besides, if you decide to fly your ballet regularly, you're going to hear that piece of music a lot.

But the music you like best, may not be the best for ballet flying. In addition to your personal taste, you have to consider what the music "does" for your ballet.

Does the music have good composition and flow? Does it create a mood? Does it provide for flying transitions and "springboards" for new maneuvers? Does it complement your flying style?

Choose your selection carefully. A piece without good flow can easily result in a disorganized or unstructured routine that is hard for others to follow. A piece that is quick and choppy may not work with slower kites or on light wind days. A piece that is too repetitive can produce a routine with no transitions or variety.

In other words, if your music is weak, your performance may be weak too. Choose well. Look for music that provides the opportunity for a broad range of different moves.

Select music that is long enough to showcase your skills, but short enough to hold people's interest. The only thing worse than a poor routine is a long, poor routine.

Start your performance when the music begins. Don't sit on the ground through a long introduction. Do something. Otherwise, people will lose interest or think things have gone wrong.

If you are interested in competition, the rule book allows for a minimum of two minutes and a maximum of four. That's a good length for most ballets - even if you aren't competing.

Composition. You want your performance to have structure. That means a beginning, a middle, and an end. Make your maneuvers clear enough that people watching can follow what you are doing. Plan for variety, but also enough repetition that you create an actual routine with continuity instead of a jumble of disorganized turns.

Transitions. The key to a good performance is moving cleanly from one strong maneuver to another. Axles, stalls, and tip stabs aren't enough. The flying between these maneuvers must have some substance too.

Transition flying is not just moving from one trick to another. Like every other part of the routine, it needs to capture some of the essence or mood of the music.

Musical Interpretation. Do the movements of the kite fit the music? Do you take advantage of the opportunities the music provides? Are you moving to the beat or flow of the music?

This is choreography. Flying to the music is the most important thing you can do. Your performance needs to reflect - or contrast - the mood and tempo that the music provides. Otherwise, you are just flying with some interesting background noise.

Execution. Finally, a good ballet needs to be flown well. Corners need to be square, circles round, and lines straight. Crashes don't add to the flow of the performance. That's why planning a complete routine is important. It allows you to practice specific moves, polish them, and perfect your timing.

Your First Ballet - *California Girls*

All this analysis still makes it sound like ballet is hard. But it isn't. Remember all those practice assignments we made you do back in Chapter 1? Did you really fly them? If so, you already have a ballet ready to go. Let's see what they look like when we fly them to music.

This first practice routine will be flown to "*California Girls*", by the Beach Boys.

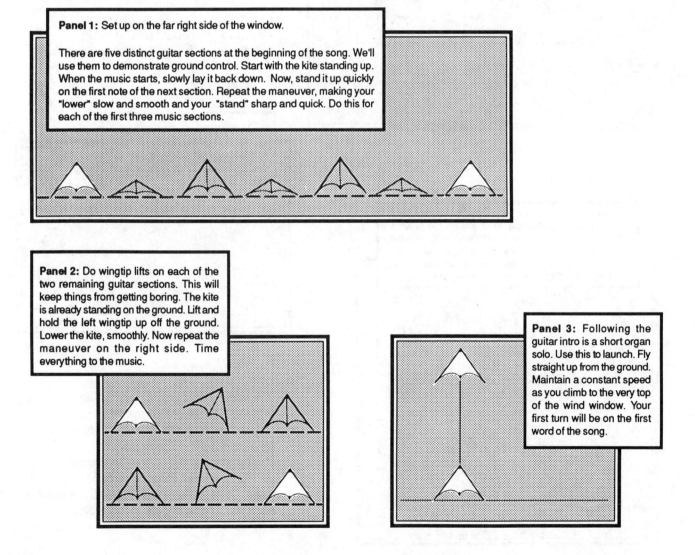

Panel 1: Set up on the far right side of the window.

There are five distinct guitar sections at the beginning of the song. We'll use them to demonstrate ground control. Start with the kite standing up. When the music starts, slowly lay it back down. Now, stand it up quickly on the first note of the next section. Repeat the maneuver, making your "lower" slow and smooth and your "stand" sharp and quick. Do this for each of the first three music sections.

Panel 2: Do wingtip lifts on each of the two remaining guitar sections. This will keep things from getting boring. The kite is already standing on the ground. Lift and hold the left wingtip up off the ground. Lower the kite, smoothly. Now repeat the maneuver on the right side. Time everything to the music.

Panel 3: Following the guitar intro is a short organ solo. Use this to launch. Fly straight up from the ground. Maintain a constant speed as you climb to the very top of the wind window. Your first turn will be on the first word of the song.

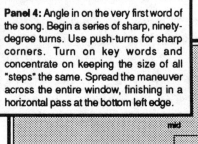

Panel 4: Angle in on the very first word of the song. Begin a series of sharp, ninety-degree turns. Use push-turns for sharp corners. Turn on key words and concentrate on keeping the size of all "steps" the same. Spread the maneuver across the entire window, finishing in a horizontal pass at the bottom left edge.

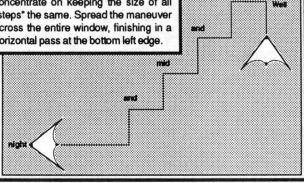

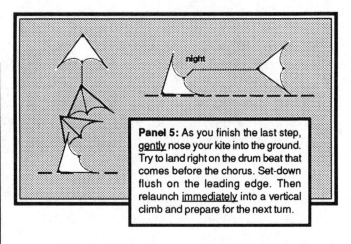

Panel 5: As you finish the last step, <u>gently</u> nose your kite into the ground. Try to land right on the drum beat that comes before the chorus. Set-down flush on the leading edge. Then relaunch <u>immediately</u> into a vertical climb and prepare for the next turn.

Panel 6: Climb quickly, then turn into a tight loop and fly out into a horizontal pass to the right. Do two more loops, each timed on key words in the chorus. Concentrate on maintaining a constant speed through the entire maneuver. Fly fast enough to finish on the right side of the window.

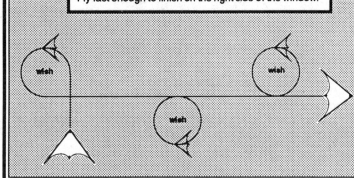

Well East Coast girls are **hip**,
I really **dig** those styles they wear.
And the Southern Girls with the way they talk,
they knock me out when I'm down there.

The **Mid**-West farmer's daughters
really **make** you feel all right,
and the Northern girls with the way they kiss,
they keep their boyfriends warm at **night**.

I **wish** they all could be California,
I **wish** they all could be California,
I **wish** they all could be California girls...

Panel 7: As the chorus fades, you have an option. You can nose land and relaunch, do a wingtip stab, or simply turn straight up into a vertical climb.

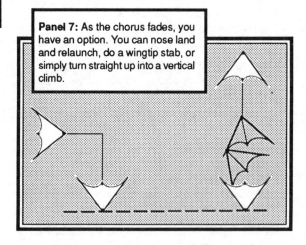

Panel 8: Climb straight up to the top of the window. Fly a tight loop and exit straight down toward the ground. Concentrate on maintaining a steady pace whether climbing or diving. Complete four loops, all exactly the same size. You want the top and bottom pairs at the same altitude, and all five lines equal distance apart.

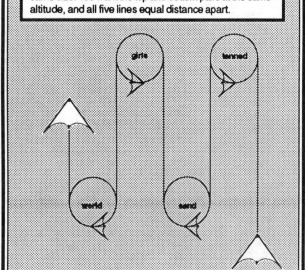

The West Coast has the sunshine
and the girls all get so **tanned.**
I dig a French bikini on the wild island dolls
by a palm tree in the **sand.**
I've been around this great big world
and I've seen all kinds of **girls.**
Yeah, but I couldn't wait to get back in the States,
back to the cutest girls in the **world.**

Panel 9: Continue the vertical climb as the second chorus begins. Do three brief stalls, equally spaced, before you turn out at the top of the window. Time the stalls to reflect the music.

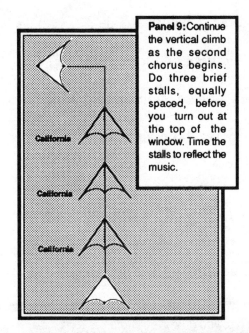

*I wish they all could be **California**,*
*I wish they all could be **California**,*
*I wish they all could be **California** girls...*

I wish they all could be California girls...
*I **wish** they all could be California girls...*
*I **wish** they all could be California girls...*
*I **wish** they all could be California girls...*

Panel 10: Wait for the organ solo that follows the chorus. As the organ begins, stall the kite and fly an axle. After you complete the axle, hold the stall until the organ ends. Then turn under and fly toward the bottom right corner.

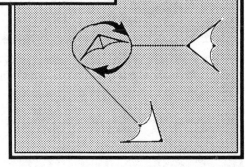

Panel 11: Continue the diagonal line. When you reach the center of the wind, turn into a small square. Time the corners to the music. Make all four sides equal and all corners perfect right-angles. Then finish the diagonal line toward the bottom right corner of the window as the chorus fades.

Panel 12: As the music fades, fly out toward the edge of the wind and execute a perfect three point landing.

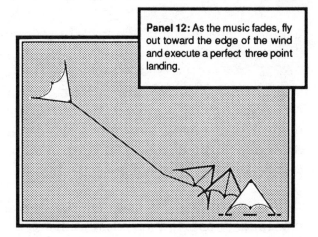

Sport kite historians tend to agree that kite ballet started in Southern California. So it's only fair that we start our first ballet lesson with music from California and the Beach Boys. Besides, "California Girls" is available on about six different albums or discs, which makes it easy to find.

The California Girls ballet is designed for fun and practice. Perform it well, and you'll produce lots of smiles on the flying field. But let's not kid ourselves that this routine is going to win first place at the Grand Nationals.

Note that drawings are not to scale.

There are several things that are important to notice about "California Girls".

The kite covers the entire wind window, from left to right and top to bottom.

You use a variety of maneuvers, including circles, angles, stalls, and ground work.

There is enough repetition for spectators to recognize the maneuvers.

Maneuvers flow from one to another with smooth transitions.

The music is upbeat and recognizable enough that spectators can anticipate moves, tricks, and transitions.

These are ballet elements that will strengthen any choreographed performance.

> *Fly big and slow, and make your transitions flow. By flying big, you give the spectators a chance to really see the move you are doing. Too often, fliers zip through a performance and people are left to wonder whether or not a maneuver was done well.*

Use Emotion to Make Your Ballet Better

Creativity and imagination make the difference between an award winning routine, and one that is, well, routine.

The primary objective of a ballet performance is entertainment. Use emotion to build the entertainment value of your routine. With emotion, you can excite people. You can inspire them. You can make them smile or even laugh out loud. And with the right touch, you can even use music and kites to bring tears to people's eyes. So let's talk about some of the emotional "tools" that are available and what you can do to create a ballet with feeling.

Anticipation. Music is often familiar or predictable. As the piece rises towards a climax or crescendo, people watching know that *something* is going to happen. Don't disappoint them. Use the opportunities that the musical selection provides to satisfy your audience.

Surprise. Shocking or surprising the audience is the easiest way to reach their emotions. When your kite is diving straight at the ground, and instead of crashing, it spins around and lands, people watching will be surprised. When your kite is nose-down on the ground, and then suddenly pops back up into the air, people will be surprised. When the kite is speeding through the air and suddenly stops in a stall, perfectly timed to a break in the music, another surprise. Surprised people are entertained people.

Grace. Make your performance elegant. Your kites are intended to be things of beauty in the air. A good ballet can communicate that beauty. Combine soft, flowing music and graceful turns. Fly maneuvers that are naturally attractive. Strive to communicate a sense of tranquility to the crowd.

Symbolism. People react to things they can relate to. Is your music a love song? Is it patriotic? Is it a familiar tune about the city you happen to be flying in? Is it associated with a film that tells a story that can easily be interpreted with your kite. Use your performance to communicate human emotions. Even the colors of your kite sail can be a symbolic tool.

Humor. Use the music in unexpected ways. Set up for a maneuver that looks predictable, and then, at the last moment, change your timing, or direction. Create an "unsolvable" problem, and then solve it. Or simply use songs with funny parts. Make people smile before you leave the field.

> *Once you have chosen your music, look for the personality of the music. Is it a cute song that tells a story, or is it a driving, aggressive piece? Does it start off slowly or quietly, and then build, or is it fairly consistent? Find a central theme or story, and then, once you've identified it, try to imagine that your kite is a puppet or marionette, and that your job is to choreograph that puppet to dance to the music you have selected.*

Second Ballet - *Come Fly with Me*

Our first practice ballet was filled with short lines, quick turns, and fast tricks. Now let's try something a bit more graceful. You'll be flying this one to "*Come Fly With Me*", by Frank Sinatra.

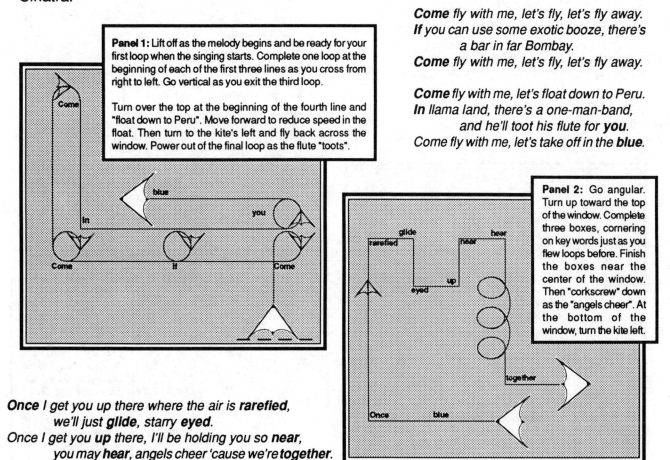

*Come fly with me, let's fly, let's fly away.
If you can use some exotic booze, there's a bar in far Bombay.
Come fly with me, let's fly, let's fly away.*

*Come fly with me, let's float down to Peru.
In llama land, there's a one-man-band, and he'll toot his flute for you.
Come fly with me, let's take off in the blue.*

Panel 1: Lift off as the melody begins and be ready for your first loop when the singing starts. Complete one loop at the beginning of each of the first three lines as you cross from right to left. Go vertical as you exit the third loop.

Turn over the top at the beginning of the fourth line and "float down to Peru". Move forward to reduce speed in the float. Then turn to the kite's left and fly back across the window. Power out of the final loop as the flute "toots".

Panel 2: Go angular. Turn up toward the top of the window. Complete three boxes, cornering on key words just as you flew loops before. Finish the boxes near the center of the window. Then "corkscrew" down as the "angels cheer". At the bottom of the window, turn the kite left.

*Once I get you up there where the air is rarefied, we'll just glide, starry eyed.
Once I get you up there, I'll be holding you so near, you may hear, angels cheer 'cause we're together.*

*Weatherwise, **It's** such a lovely day.*
*Just say the **words** and we'll beat the birds*
*   down to Acapulco Bay.*
*It's **perfect** for a flying honeymoon **they** say.*
*Come fly with me, let's fly, let's **fly away**.*

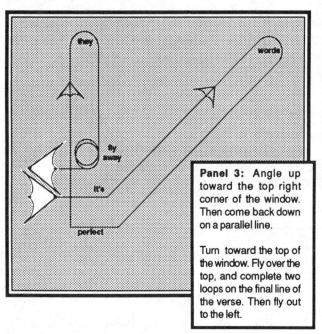

Panel 3: Angle up toward the top right corner of the window. Then come back down on a parallel line.

Turn toward the top of the window. Fly over the top, and complete two loops on the final line of the verse. Then fly out to the left.

Once I get you up there where the air is rarefied,
*   we'll just glide, starry eyed.*
*Once I get you up there, **I'll** be holding you so near,*
*   you may hear, **angels** cheer 'cause we're together*

*Weatherwise, it's such a lovely **day**.*
*You just **say** the words and we'll beat **the** birds*
*   down to Acapulco Bay.*
*It's **perfect** for a flying honeymoon **they** say.*
*Come fly with me, let's **fly**, let's fly.*
***Pack up** let's fly away.*

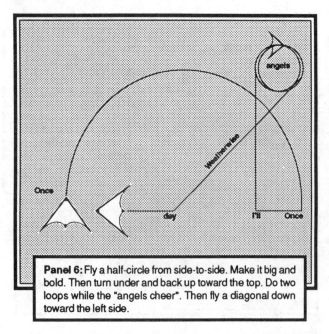

Panel 6: Fly a half-circle from side-to-side. Make it big and bold. Then turn under and back up toward the top. Do two loops while the "angels cheer". Then fly a diagonal down toward the left side.

Panel 4: The next two panels cover an instrumental section. Time the turns to match the musical "springboards".

Not all sides of this "split diamond" are the same length but the corners are each ninety-degree angles. Fly it carefully.

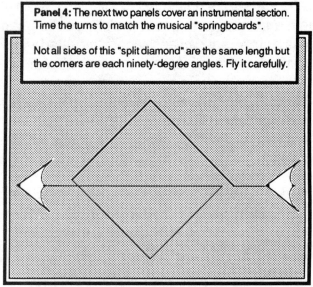

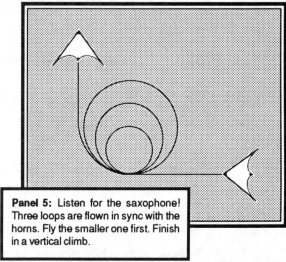

Panel 5: Listen for the saxophone! Three loops are flown in sync with the horns. Fly the smaller one first. Finish in a vertical climb.

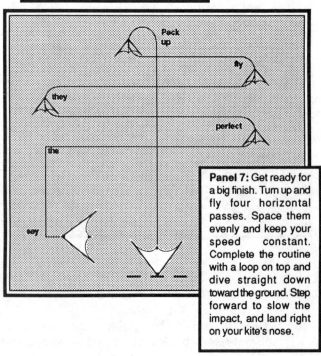

Panel 7: Get ready for a big finish. Turn up and fly four horizontal passes. Space them evenly and keep your speed constant. Complete the routine with a loop on top and dive straight down toward the ground. Step forward to slow the impact, and land right on your kite's nose.

Come Fly With Me is taken from the Capitol album and disc of the same name. Don't substitute the Duets II disc. The arrangement and even wording is different. Again, not all diagrams are drawn to scale. Panel notes should help you decide how big to fly the maneuvers.

This routine is quite different from the previous one. The musical style is different, and so is the flying style. The song has a theme you can work with.

Come Fly With Me is a good example of how to use humor to get people smiling. Like any joke, the effectiveness wears down if it is told too often. But the song also carries a sense of timeless finesse and grace that has made it a classic. Adapt the lessons of this routine to your own musical taste. By relying on big, flowing maneuvers, your performance can be classic too.

Advanced Design Tricks

Start strong. Most people watching will decide if they like what they see in the first thirty seconds of your ballet. Don't save all the best stuff for the ending. Use your music, and your opening moves to make an impression right at the beginning of your performance. Include some creative ground work. Make sure your first maneuvers are among your best. Get the crowd behind you right away.

Use maneuvers that look hard. Figures or tricks that are hard to execute but look easy don't add to your routine. You may impress the other fliers, but most spectators and even some judges won't know the difference. Your timing or execution will need to be perfect just to avoid a mistake, and flaws will be more obvious. So unless you have practiced that fancy new move enough that you know you can get it every time, leave it out. Use maneuvers that look difficult, but aren't really that hard to perform. Rely on illusion, not luck.

Look at things from the spectator's point of view. Spectators don't always understand what they are watching. And often, part of the crowd can't see the whole routine. A maneuver that looks like a crash and recovery may be interpreted as a lucky "save" instead of a brilliantly planned ground move. Turns at the bottom outside edge of the field may be beyond people's view. Use the crowd's perceptions to your advantage.

Plan your transitions. Transitions need to be more than just flying between stunts and maneuvers. They need to look like maneuvers themselves and they need to be smooth and brief enough to hold people's interest. If necessary, rearrange your routine to fix any transitional problems and make things flow.

Always act like you flew great. If you look like you were happy with your performance, people will believe it went well. If you look unhappy, spectators will wonder what went wrong. Besides, just because you know you have flown better, doesn't mean these folks have ever seen better.

Save something for a big finish. People love to see the kite land perfectly timed to the last note of the music. A crisp and creative finale makes the performance look more polished. And remember, judges will be writing down a score right after you are done. Give them something to think about that may overcome any minor problems in the middle of the routine.

Third Ballet - *Wizards and Warriors*

All of the music we have chosen so far for our practice ballets has contained words.

Songs with words are helpful because we can use those words to tell us when to turn. But often, lyrical music is not the best choice for ballet. The tunes can be repetitive or lack the kind of variety that allows a lot of different types of kite maneuvers. Classical music and movie soundtracks are a good alternative.

Soundtracks are designed to generate emotions and often provide interesting changes in tempo and style. And that's exactly what you're looking for in a good ballet. For our final practice ballet, we'll try the theme to an old television show called "*Wizards and Warriors*".

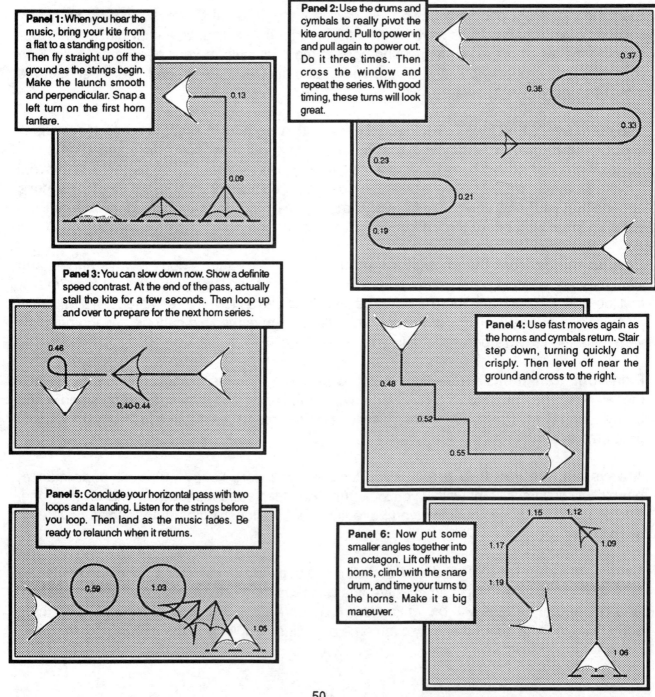

Panel 1: When you hear the music, bring your kite from a flat to a standing position. Then fly straight up off the ground as the strings begin. Make the launch smooth and perpendicular. Snap a left turn on the first horn fanfare.

Panel 2: Use the drums and cymbals to really pivot the kite around. Pull to power in and pull again to power out. Do it three times. Then cross the window and repeat the series. With good timing, these turns will look great.

Panel 3: You can slow down now. Show a definite speed contrast. At the end of the pass, actually stall the kite for a few seconds. Then loop up and over to prepare for the next horn series.

Panel 4: Use fast moves again as the horns and cymbals return. Stair step down, turning quickly and crisply. Then level off near the ground and cross to the right.

Panel 5: Conclude your horizontal pass with two loops and a landing. Listen for the strings before you loop. Then land as the music fades. Be ready to relaunch when it returns.

Panel 6: Now put some smaller angles together into an octagon. Lift off with the horns, climb with the snare drum, and time your turns to the horns. Make it a big maneuver.

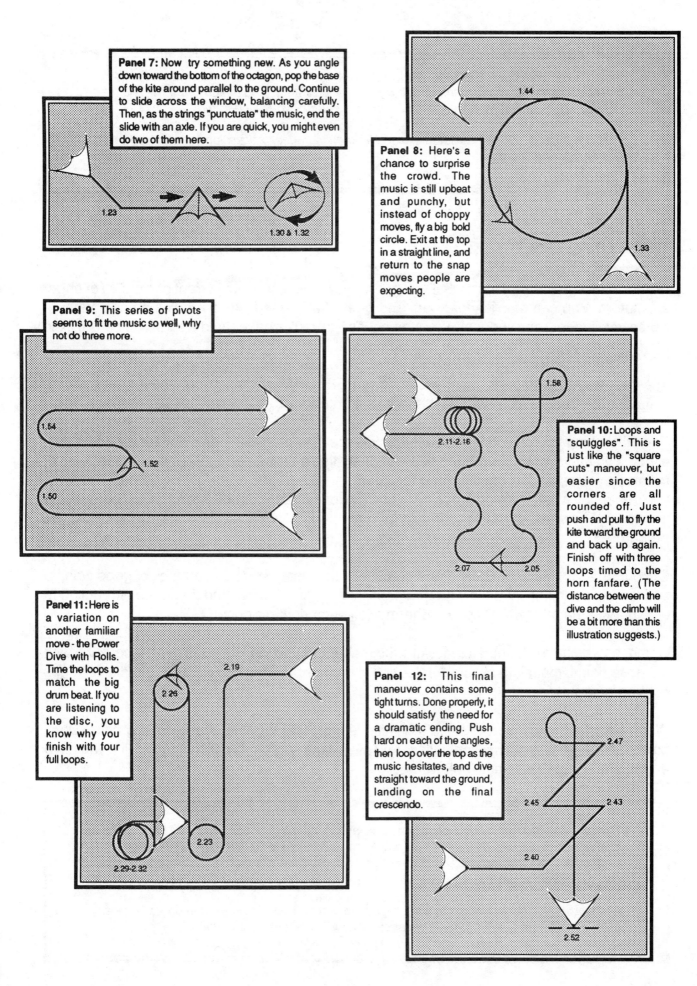

Panel 7: Now try something new. As you angle down toward the bottom of the octagon, pop the base of the kite around parallel to the ground. Continue to slide across the window, balancing carefully. Then, as the strings "punctuate" the music, end the slide with an axle. If you are quick, you might even do two of them here.

Panel 8: Here's a chance to surprise the crowd. The music is still upbeat and punchy, but instead of choppy moves, fly a big bold circle. Exit at the top in a straight line, and return to the snap moves people are expecting.

Panel 9: This series of pivots seems to fit the music so well, why not do three more.

Panel 10: Loops and "squiggles". This is just like the "square cuts" maneuver, but easier since the corners are all rounded off. Just push and pull to fly the kite toward the ground and back up again. Finish off with three loops timed to the horn fanfare. (The distance between the dive and the climb will be a bit more than this illustration suggests.)

Panel 11: Here is a variation on another familiar move - the Power Dive with Rolls. Time the loops to match the big drum beat. If you are listening to the disc, you know why you finish with four full loops.

Panel 12: This final maneuver contains some tight turns. Done properly, it should satisfy the need for a dramatic ending. Push hard on each of the angles, then loop over the top as the music hesitates, and dive straight toward the ground, landing on the final crescendo.

51

Wizards and Warriors was a short-lived TV show that never made it to the big screen. You can find its swashbuckling theme music on "The Great Fantasy Adventure Album" (Telark CD-80342). Note that we have used CD track times to tell you when to turn.

This is a great disc for kite ballet music and features parades, processions, and attacks from twenty different shows.

When Things Go Wrong

"Performance Fever" -- That's what you get when you first step out in front of a crowd of eager spectators. You can practice for hours and be REALLY good. But try it with an audience, or worse yet, judges, and suddenly you start acting like you've never held a sport kite before. And at that point, you can do some of the dumbest things!

The best way to cure performance fever is to PERFORM. Some people never get over the stage fright - but the more you do it, the less it bothers you.

The other thing you can do to increase confidence is to practice. Don't wait for a perfect day, either. You may want optimal conditions for designing a ballet, perfecting a new maneuver, or to firm-up your skills. But the best time for a general rehearsal is in marginal weather. That way, you'll be ready when the wind drops off to nothing, or suddenly doubles in force just before your turn to fly. The weather never seems to be quite perfect when you fly in front of a crowd. Be prepared.

Of course, all the self-confidence and practice in the world won't do you a bit of good when a sudden wind lull drops your low ground pass into the dirt. You're standing there, struggling to get your kite up off the ground, and the music keeps right on going.

Or maybe you have planned a fancy ground maneuver and the kite flops over, face down with the nose pointing straight at you. A relaunch is impossible. And like we said, the music keeps right on going.

When disaster strikes, and eventually it will, the first thing to remember is to stay calm. Don't panic. There is a way out of every mess. And even if the way out is difficult, acting like you have a problem just makes things look worse.

The rulebook requires a small penalty if you crash, but a much larger one if you fail to finish a routine with the music. So unless it is completely impossible to fly, get your kite back into the air and finish what you started. Make the best of it. You'll feel better about your performance, and so will your audience.

Afterwards, give some thought to what happened and how you could have improved things. Always learn from a bad situation, because there will surely be a next time.

In competition, an unplanned ground touch results in a small penalty. If you crash in ballet, you get the same penalty whether you relaunch yourself or get help from someone else. The difference is that struggling to relaunch in a bad situation may mean dragging the kite across the field a bit. You can tangle a line and make the crash worse. You can relaunch with a tangled line or loose spar and crash again. Or worst of all, you can break something while dragging into a good position to lift off.

Plan on having some help positioned on or around the field. We call them "ground crew". And unless your crash is really easy to recover from, use your crew. They can unwrap tangled lines, insert loose spars, tie broken lines, and even make some minor on-field repairs.

When a kite goes down, everyone watching hopes for a relaunch. The sympathy of the crowd is with you. You may get louder applause for recovering from a bad crash, then for flying the maneuver you planned in the first place.

In the moment it takes for your crew to reach the kite and check it over, stop and think. Use the situation to your advantage. Are you standing in the best place for a relaunch? Should you take this opportunity to move the kite deeper in the field on light wind days? Is there a good way for you to get smoothly back into your routine?

Like we said before, the music keeps right on going. No matter how fast you fly your routine, you are never going to catch up. And while you are trying to catch up, everything you do will be out of sync with the music.

If you can't slide gracefully back into the routine, fly into position for an upcoming maneuver and wait there. Improvise. Do _something_ that matches the music. Your unplanned moves may look better than what you planned in the first place.

When things go wrong, the person who stays calm and then reacts will come out ahead.

When you enter a formal event, you are required to perform inside the boundaries of the contest field. The size of the field may vary at different contests, but the rules are -- if you or your kite go out of bounds, you get disqualified.

It doesn't matter if the winds are light. You aren't allowed to back up off the field to stay airborne. If the winds are strong and you get pulled out -- too bad... In competition, you have to do it in the flagged-off field. Period.

Think about safety whenever you fly. Even in informal demonstrations, it's a good idea to keep the kites, and the spectators a safe distance apart.

Chapter 5: More Magical Maneuvers:
Advanced Precision Figures

Advanced maneuvers are made up from the same curves, angles, and lines as more simple figures. The difference is that there may be more of those turns, or that they may come closer together. Don't panic. Just because they are more complicated, doesn't mean they are more difficult. Just break the figures down into their easier components.

The secret to flying complex maneuvers well is to fly them slowly. Give yourself time to think and react. It's not like there is a time limit or anything.

The other secret is to study the illustrations carefully. Are lines the same length or loops the same size? Do you pass over the same point in the window repeatedly? Are several dives parallel to each other, or perpendicular to a horizontal pass?

Look for tools that you can use in the sky or on the ground. Clouds, trees, or even the posts marking your flying field can help you position figures. It's these small things that make your performance look "advanced".

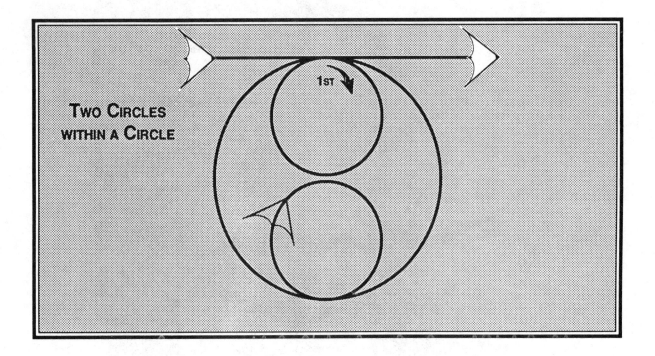

Two Circles within a Circle: This is a good maneuver for pull turns. The key is smooth transitions between the small circles and the bigger one. Focus on an imaginary vertical center of the window and arrange all your flying around that line.

Remember to move forward as you dive, and back as you climb. Keep a steady, even pace throughout the entire maneuver, and don't be rushed. Remember that the larger circle will be flown through the entire range of wind changes in the window. Switching from smaller to larger arcs may tempt you to fly the smaller circles faster. Don't do it.

One common mistake is to fly the outside circle too narrow. Make it round, not oval.

Concentrate on flying both the smaller circles the same size and space them carefully. They can "touch" in the center of the window, but not overlap. If you form the top one too big, you'll end up with a noticeable spacing error.

Start with a high horizontal pass toward the left. Turn up and over to get high in the window, straighten your flight, and call "IN" about half way back to the center.

Maintain straight and smooth flight. When you reach the center of the window, pull with your right. Anticipate the turn so you can hit it <u>right on</u> the center line.

Fly the smaller circle first. Make it perfectly round, with the bottom arc passing just over the exact center of the window. Move forward on the dive, move back to increase power on the climb. As you return to the top, shift into the larger circle. Your objective is a smooth transition with no bumps, angles, or jerks. Just ease up gently on your pull turn.

To keep the outer circle properly rounded, fly well out to the right. Notice that the outside edges of the big circle are as far left and right of center as where you start and finish the maneuver.

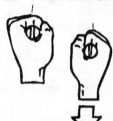

KEEP TRANSITIONS SMOOTH

As you return to the centerline at the bottom of the window, prepare to fly the second small circle. Again, anticipate the turn so you can hit it <u>right on</u> the center line and directly below the first one. Now, focus on making the bottom circle exactly the same size as the upper one. The top should be just below the exact center of the window.

PULL-RIGHT FOR THE SMALL CIRCLE

As you fly under again, ease out to complete the second half of the big circle. Move back during this long arcing climb. Then as you return to the top of the window, intersect the highest point of the smaller circle at the vertical center of the window and straighten out by bringing your hands together.

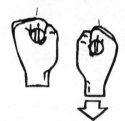

Make your exit pass the same length as your entrance, and call "OUT". **PULL-RIGHT LESS FOR THE BIG CIRCLE**

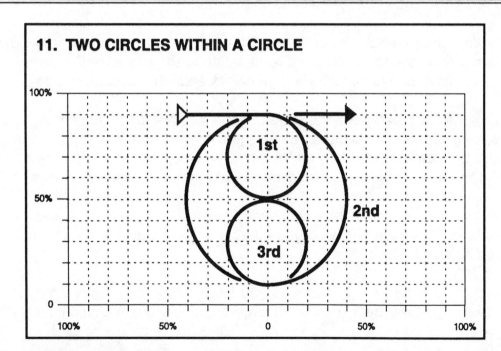

11. TWO CIRCLES WITHIN A CIRCLE

Competition Spacing: *IN and OUT are called forty percent from the center of the window at an altitude of ninety percent. The small circles have a diameter of forty percent. The large circle has an eighty percent diameter. The bottom of the large circle is ten percent off the ground. Note that IN and OUT are called at the same distance from center as the extreme outside edges of the large circle.*

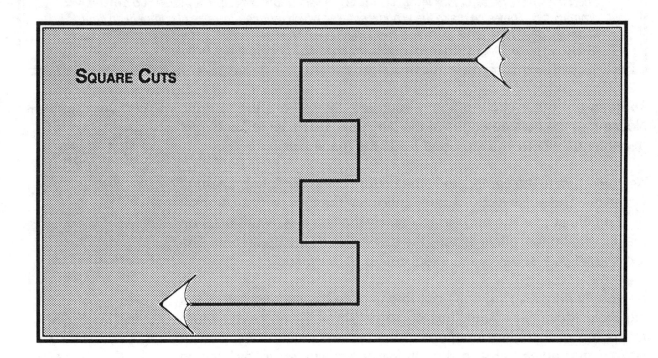

Square Cuts: This is the kind of maneuver that you can't think too hard about. It contains eight quick sharp corners. Everything happens too fast. Watch the kite and turn; watch and turn again. If you blink, you'll miss something important.

In stronger winds, you will need to move forward through the whole maneuver to slow things down to a manageable speed. Most of the turns come in the center of the power zone. In lighter winds, you may need to move back to generate enough pressure for sharp turns.

Notice that all of the lines, except for the entrance and exit, are the same length. Each "box" has the same height and width, so divide the height of your window into four parts, and make each step that size. But remember that your kite will fly vertical lines much faster than horizontal ones. This means you will need to anticipate and react faster when you push from horizontal.

Start with a vertical climb on the outside right edge. Turn in at the top and stabilize your flight. Because you are at the edge of the wind, you may need to back up to generate more speed. When you are half way to the center, call "IN".

Have you divided the window in quarters so you know what size to make your steps? A common mistake is to make the first ones too large and to run out of space later.

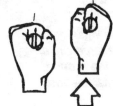 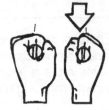 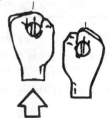 

PUSH-RIGHT TO PIVOT LEFT **RECOVER AND FLY STRAIGHT** **PUSH-LEFT TO PIVOT RIGHT** **RECOVER AND FLY STRAIGHT**

Push-right for the first corner. The nose of the kite will pivot toward the ground. Hesitate for a micro-second, and then push-right again. This will turn you back to the right on your first short horizontal pass. Anticipate, and then push-left. You have just finished your first box. Only three more to go.

Quick! Push-left to go horizontal. If you are on track, this pass will fly through the direct centerpoint of the window. If you are too low, you better start worrying about hitting the ground.

Anticipate. Your objective is to turn vertical on the same line as your first dive. Now push-right. Hesitate, and push-right again to go horizontal.

This is the time when you need to decide if you are in position, or flying too low. If you're in position, then two more left push-turns will complete the final box. But if you are too low, consider an extra hard push that will reverse your direction. Better to mess up the spacing of the bottom box - or even eliminate the corners all together, then to crash and lose all points. Worse yet, you might damage your kite. Better decide fast!

Your final push should turn the kite toward the left side of the window. Focus on flying straight and smooth again. Think about your speed. Maintain a slight tension on the upper flying line to offset the kite's tendency to drift toward the ground.

Fly out, half way to the left edge, and call "OUT".

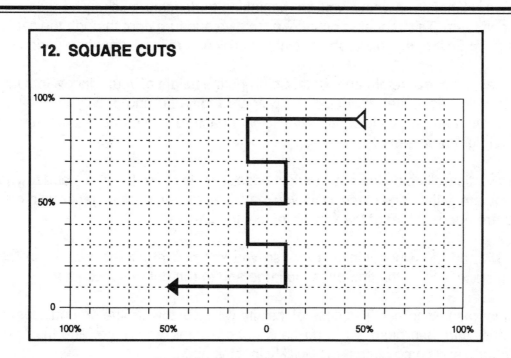

12. SQUARE CUTS

Competition Spacing: IN is called fifty percent right of center at an altitude of ninety percent. The first step down is ten percent left of center. Each subsequent line is twenty percent high or twenty percent long. The midpoint of the third horizontal is the exact center of the wind window.

The final horizontal is sixty percent long. OUT is called fifty percent left of center at an altitude of ten percent.

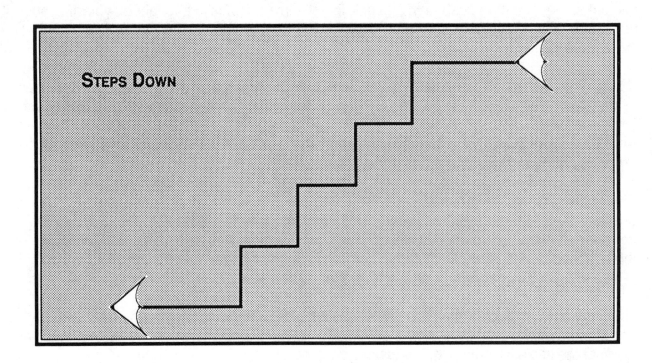

STEPS DOWN

Steps Down: Hopefully, by now, you are beginning to develop quick flying reflexes. You're going to need them. This maneuver continues to dive and turn right through the center of the power zone. To do it right, you'll require eight sharp corners in a very short period of time.

Each step has the same height and width. So divide the height of your window into four parts, and plan to make each step that size. Be prepared for wind and gravity to force your kite down and stretch out the vertical dives. Anticipate each turn and begin a moment early, so you can turn right on the mark.

Start with a vertical climb on the outside right edge. Turn in at the top and stabilize your flight. Because you are at the edge of the wind, you may need to step back to generate more speed. When you are about a third of the way to the center, call "IN".

Have you divided the window in quarters so you know what size to make your steps? A common mistake is to fly the first ones too large and to run out of space later.

Push-right for the first corner. The nose of the kite will pivot toward the ground. Hesitate for a micro-second, and then push-left to go back to horizontal. Anticipate, and then push-right again. The turns will come almost too quickly to think about.

Count off each step as you complete it. If you are on track, the third horizontal leg will pass through the direct centerpoint of the window. Two more to go.

Be careful when you are close to the ground, and whatever you do, <u>don't crash</u>.

A "crash" is defined as a collision with the ground which brings the kite to a full stop. Wingtip scrapes, unintended midair stalls, and ground maneuvers that never get off the ground are problems -- but technically not crashes.

In a precision competition, a crash results in a zero score. Other unintentional ground contact also results in a penalty, but a much smaller one.

Many precision maneuvers place you uncomfortably close to the bottom of the window. Practice to gain confidence and skill in low altitude passes. Be prepared for lulls in the wind or bumps in the terrain that reach up and grab at your kite. Learn to avoid ground contact unless you are planning to land.

Push-right - hesitate - push-left. Push-right - hesitate - push-left. Finish the fourth step and turn horizontal just above the ground. Resist the temptation to turn again.

Keep your flight straight and smooth now. Fly out to one third from the edge, and call "OUT".

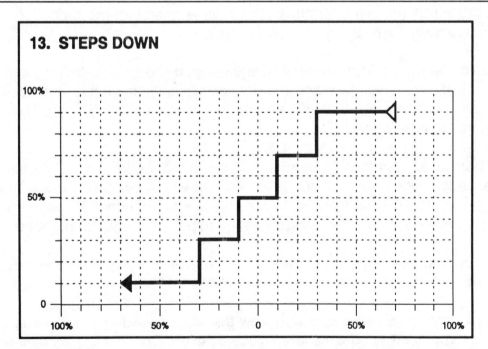

13. STEPS DOWN

Competition Spacing: IN is called seventy percent right of center at an altitude of ninety percent. The first step down is thirty percent right of center.

Each subsequent step is twenty percent high and twenty percent long. The midpoint of the third horizontal is the exact center of the wind window.

The final horizontal is forty percent long. OUT is called seventy percent left of center at an altitude of ten percent.

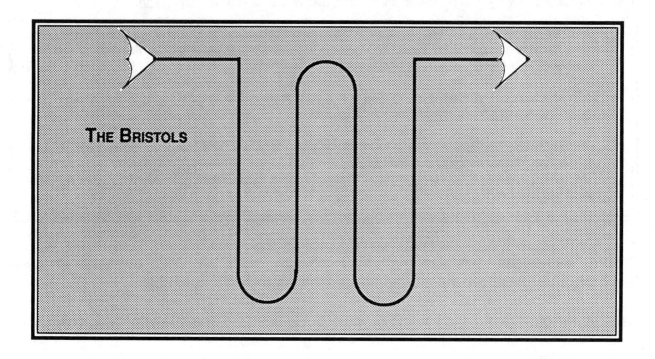

The Bristols: Here is another opportunity to combine push-turns and pull-turns into one maneuver. Remember, push for angles, pull for curves.

Notice that all of the vertical lines are equal distance apart. Also notice that the center turn is at the same altitude as the entrance and exit passes. It's common on this maneuver to fly the middle turn too low, or to make the vertical lines too close together. Be careful, also, not to oversteer on any of your curves.

Start with a horizontal pass from the right side flying out to the left edge. This will give you one last chance to check the speed of the kite and put you in the best position to begin the maneuver. Turn up and over to start the high pass back to the right. About half way to the center, call "IN". Make sure you are flying straight and right at the top of the window.

About a one-fourth of the way out from the center, push-left. Make it a good, crisp, ninety-degree corner.

Once you turn, start to move forward and slow the kite's speed. If you have started on a straight line, all you need to do is keep your hands even. Concentrate on maintaining the same pace that you started the maneuver with.

Three fourths of the way through the dive, stop moving forward. Tension the flying lines and store some power for the turn that is coming. Then, as you approach the ground, pull with your left hand to start the turn. As you come about, pull even with your right hand and step back. Use that extra thrust to climb vertically. Remember, pulling powers you into the turn, pulling again powers you out of it.

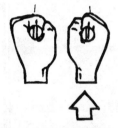

Be careful not to oversteer. Start releasing from the turn <u>before</u> the spine of your kite has come perpendicular to the ground again. Make sure that your vertical climb is exactly parallel to the vertical dive.

The next turn comes high in the sky, so continue to step back as you climb. Move fast enough to maintain thrust, but not so fast that your kite is flying faster than in the dive. Then, as you approach the top of the window, begin your pull-turn to the right. Continue to step back to maintain power. The peak of the turn should be on the direct centerline of the wind window.

When you come over the top, begin to move forward again. Instead of pulling left to straighten, try pushing right. This will reduce power as you start to dive. At the same time, you can step forward to slow the kite and maintain the same pace as in the climb. Now all you need to do is fly another turn near the ground, exactly like the first one. If your spacing is correct, your final vertical climb will be a fourth of the way right of center.

Fly back up to the top of the window, and when you are level with your first horizontal pass, push-left to turn right. Continue your straight flight and as you reach the halfway point to the edge, call "OUT". Now catch your breath, and after the event, go ask the judges if they know why this maneuver is called the Bristols. It's an interesting story.

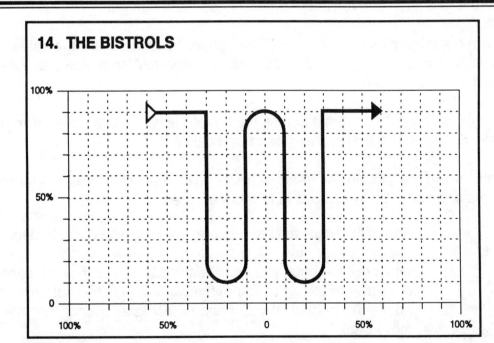

14. THE BISTROLS

Competition Spacing: IN and OUT are called forty percent from the outside edges at an altitude of ninety percent. Corner turns are each thirty percent from center. All vertical lines are twenty percent apart. The reverse turns are ten percent high and twenty percent wide. Bottom turns are both ten percent off the ground. The top turn is at ninety percent altitude, and peaks directly on the centerline of the window.

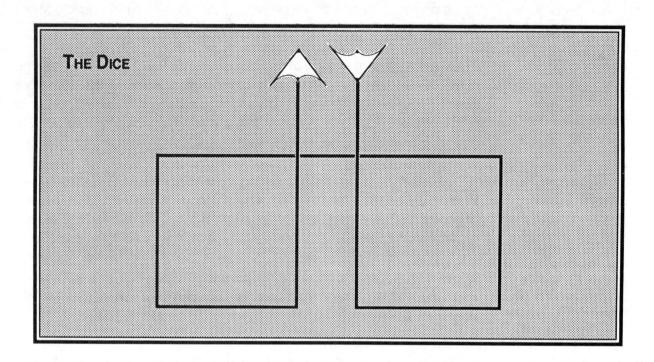

The Dice: That top horizontal pass goes a long, long way across the window and right through the power zone too. Close to the ground, you have a reference point for long passes. But higher in the sky, you need to concentrate to keep them straight.

Look closely at the proportions of the figure. The bottom horizontals are the same length as the side verticals. That's the key to keeping the boxes square. Also notice that every corner in the figure is a turn to the left.

Start high on the left edge. Fly straight across the top of the window and then turn down just right of center. Snap the kite toward the ground and call "IN".

Track straight toward the ground. As in any vertical dive, your objective is to minimize any side movement and pace yourself. Move in to reduce speed.

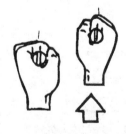

**PUSH-RIGHT FOR
90 DEGREE LEFT TURNS**

As you approach the ground, prepare for the best ninety-degree corner you have ever flown. Anticipate the turn, then punch your right hand forward. The result you want is a sharp corner that will send the kite back toward the right side of the window with the bottom wingtip just above the ground. If you need to increase speed near the ground, move back.

Fly out just beyond the center of the right side of the window and prepare to punch the kite into another vertical. Make a careful mental note of the length of this ground pass. Then punch again with your right to pivot the nose of the kite up and fly the exact same distance before you turn again. You've got this first box nailed!

Now you have to deal with that long horizontal pass. Keep your hands steady to avoid any shaking or "wobbles". As you know, gravity always tries to pull you toward the ground on long passes. Maintain a slight "up" pressure by holding your right hand slightly back from the left. Use your feet to adjust speed as you move in and out of the power zone.

HOLD BACK SLIGHTLY ON THE RIGHT TO MAINTAIN A LEVEL HORIZONTAL PASS

When you have flown just past the half-way point on the left side of the window, push-right to turn down. This second box should mirror the first one. Just remember to keep all of your lines the same length as that first horizontal pass. Turn left, just above the ground. Then turn left again as you approach center. Move forward during dives, move back during passes and climbs.

The final climb is parallel to the dive you used at the beginning of the maneuver. Don't rush things now. Maintain your pace right through to the top of the window. When you get there, call "OUT" and turn to either the left or right.

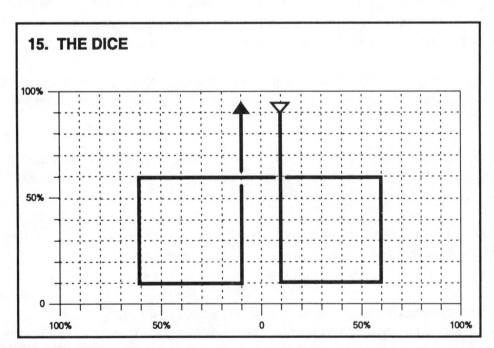

15. THE DICE

Competition Spacing: IN and OUT are called at an altitude of ninety percent. Inside vertical lines are ten percent from center. Outside verticals are sixty percent from center.

Lower horizontals are ten percent off the ground. The long horizontal is sixty percent above the ground.

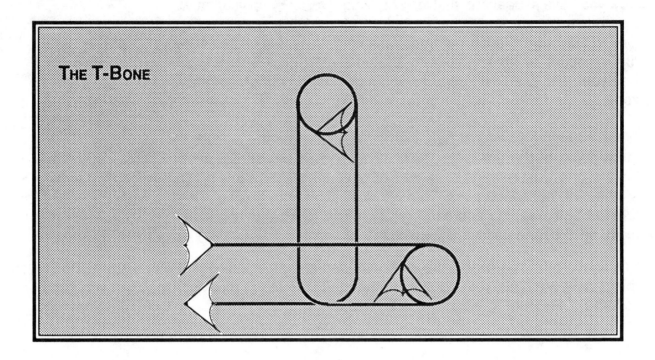

THE T-BONE

The T-Bone: This is a busy figure with lots of short passes and right turns. Fly the horizontal part first, then turn up for the vertical part which is right in the middle of the window.

Notice that the two circles require you to actually fly one-and-a-half revolutions. Take them slow and be careful not to oversteer. Watch the nose of your kite and anticipate when to pull out.

Start with a long ground pass from the right. At the left edge of the window, pull-right to curve up and over. Try to position your kite at an altitude of about one-third and straighten out as you fly back. Call "IN" half way to the center.

Keep parallel to the ground as you pass through the middle of the window and prepare yourself for the first turn. A third of the way past center, pull-right and begin your revolutions.

It's important to remember that these are not true spins, but instead, small circles. Don't be tempted to turn your kite on its wingtip. Trace the outside edge of the turn a second time as you come around and prepare to start your second horizontal pass.

PULL-RIGHT THE
SAME AMOUNT TO KEEP
CIRCLES AND CURVES
IDENTICAL IN SIZE

The second pass is short and close to the ground. Move back to compensate for the lighter winds there. Then start to curve up at exactly the center of the window. Pull-right with the same force that you used in the circle, but ease out of the turn quickly to produce a smooth arc that sends your kite straight up and perpendicular to the ground.

Keep moving back to maintain a constant speed as you climb. As you approach the top of the window, begin your second circle. Proportions here are tricky, but it may help to remember that the maneuver is slightly wider than it is tall.

Make your second circle the same size as the first one, and as you pass over the top a second time, ease the kite into a vertical dive. Start to move forward now to keep things slow.

Stop moving as you approach the ground, and tension your lines for the final turn. Pull-right. Ease the kite onto exactly the same line that you were flying in the first part of this bottom pass. Now fly straight and parallel out to the left and call "OUT" right below where you started.

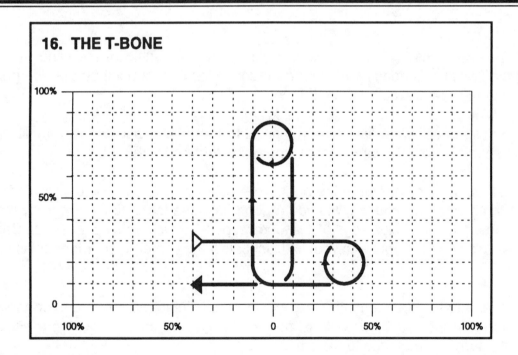

16. THE T-BONE

Competition Spacing: *All parallel lines are twenty percent apart. Circles are similarly twenty percent in diameter.*

The figure begins and ends forty percent left of center. The entrance line is at an altitude of thirty percent, and the exit line is at ten percent. The lower circle extends forty-five percent to the right.

Vertical lines are balanced about the center of the window and the upper circle peaks at an altitude of eighty-five percent.

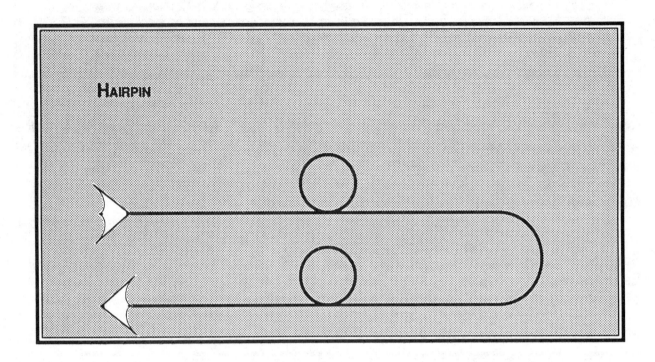

Hairpin: The two spins in this figure start right on the centerline of the wind. In fact, the middle of the first spin is dead center in the window. Identify that point before you begin and resolve to put the spins exactly where they belong.

Position yourself deep in the field. You will need to be moving back constantly to maintain power and speed in both the long passes and quick turns near the edge.

Start with a long ground pass from the right. This is exactly the same line you will fly to exit later, so using it as an approach gives you a good final chance to test both horizontal flying and the reverse turn. At the left edge of the window, pull-right to curve up and over. Bring your left hand even to straighten out with your kite just below the center of the window. As you level off, call "IN".

Your objective is to maintain smooth, straight flight, parallel to the ground, even though you are going to interrupt it at the middle of the window with a spin. Check your speed, and anticipate the turn as you come to the center line.

At exactly the center of the window, turn your kite into the spin. Pull back with your left, and if you need to make the circle smaller, push with your right at the same time.

Be careful not to make the circles too small. Consider the size of the maneuver carefully, and compare the size of your kite to the proportions of the spin. They should fill nearly a quarter of the height of the window.

USE A COMBINATION PUSH-PULL FOR TIGHTER LOOPS

Unless the window is quite compressed, the kite will not be turning inside its own wingtip.

Now continue your horizontal pass to the right. As you approach the edge, pull-pull to turn under and reverse direction. Use the same kind of turn you practiced to enter the maneuver. Power in, and power out. Your objective is to be flying back to the left in a straight line just above the ground.

As always, you need to be careful in low passes to avoid any ground touches. The winds are lighter here so you will need to keep moving back to increase speed and power.

As you return to the center of the window, time your second spin so it is directly below the first one in the center of the wind. Pull-right this time. Make both circles exactly the same size. The temptation will be to spin the kite fast so the wind roars off the sail. Don't do it! Timing your exit is crucial, and slower movements allow more precise calculations.

As you finish the second circle, all you need to do is continue the bottom horizontal to the right edge of the window and call "OUT".

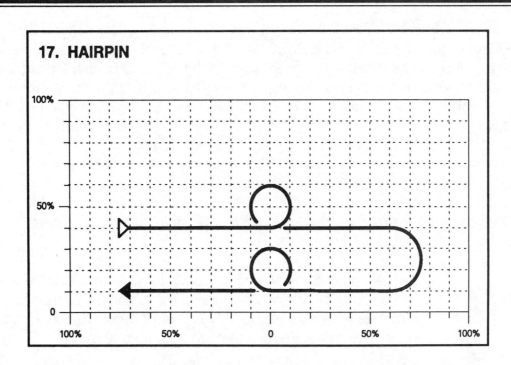

17. HAIRPIN

Competition Spacing: IN and OUT are thirty percent in from the left edge. The first pass is at forty percent altitude with the first circle flown at the center of the window. Circles are twenty percent tall.

The reverse turn is ten percent wide and thirty percent tall.

The bottom horizontal is at ten percent altitude with the second or lower circle placed in the middle of the window.

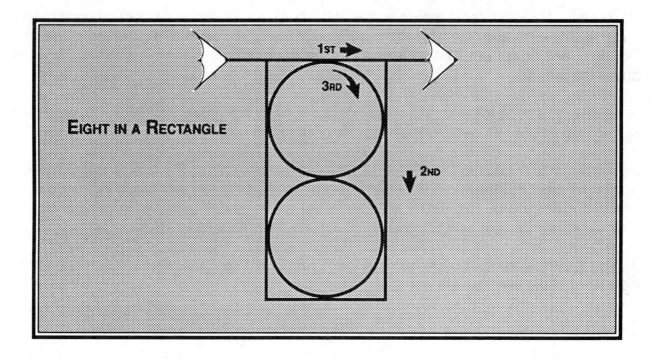

Eight in a Rectangle: The rectangle is flown first, then the circles. Let's be clear about that right off the top. Also notice that this is a "true" figure eight made of connected circles, rather than the teardrop-shaped transitions that you have seen before. In order to fit two perfect circles neatly inside, the rectangle must be exactly twice as tall as it is wide. Got it? Good, now let's fly it.

Start with a high horizontal pass toward the left. Turn up and over to get higher in the window, straighten your flight, and call "IN" about half way back to the center.

Fly straight across the top of the window. About a quarter of the way past center, push-left to turn down.

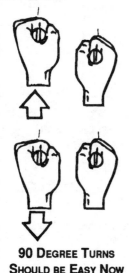

90 Degree Turns Should be Easy Now

Angular push-turns should be coming easily now. Use them to fly all of the rectangle and concentrate on proportions. Remember, you want it half as wide as it is tall. Move forward during the dive, move back during the climb. Keep your pace smooth and even.

As you finish the fourth turn, get ready to fly the circles. The first curve will come quickly.

Pull-right to curve down. The hard part will be to space the first circle so the outside edge passes exactly over the border of the rectangle. Continue to pull-right as you turn under. Then begin your transition to the second circle in the exact midpoint of the window. Pull-left to begin to curve back.

Any spacing errors will be easy to see at the base of the maneuver. Make sure the bottom of the circle, and the bottom of the rectangle are the same height above the ground. Then continue to curve around so that you switch back to the top circle at the center of the window again.

Anticipate the turn so you can hit it <u>right on</u> the center point.

Concentrate on staying inside the lines of the rectangle. As you reach the top of the circle, straighten out your flight so you are simply continuing the line you created when you started the maneuver. Fly across the top of the window and call "OUT" when you are about halfway to the right edge.

With all of these dives, climbs, curves and turns, maintaining an even pace may be a problem. Practice moving forward and back as you fly each part. Spacing and proportion are the most important things to worry about.

Try flying the maneuver as slowly as possible. You'll be surprised how much difference a few extra seconds makes.

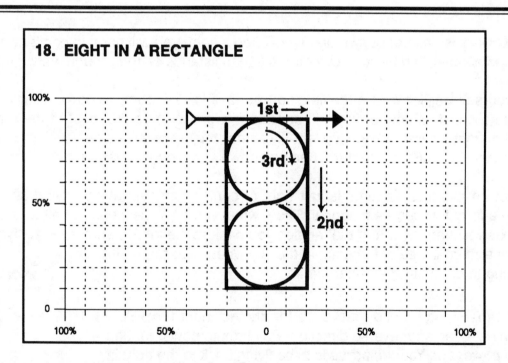

18. EIGHT IN A RECTANGLE

Competition Spacing: IN is called on a straight line forty percent left of center at an altitude of ninety percent. The rectangle is forty percent wide and eighty percent tall. This leaves the bottom of the maneuver ten percent off the ground.

The figure eight is comprised of two equal circles, each forty percent in diameter. The circles fit completely inside the rectangle.

OUT is called forty percent right of center.

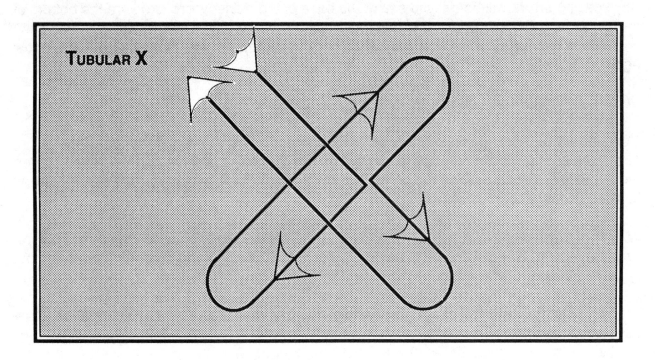

Tubular X: Here is another busy maneuver. To do it right, you will need to concentrate, keep all your lines parallel, and fly your lower turns equal distance off the ground. Let's give it a try.

Position yourself well forward in the field so you have lots of room. To power your turns, and to maintain a constant speed, you will need to move back through most of the maneuver. Start in a horizontal pass from the top left. Fly across the top of the window until you are about a quarter of the way out from center. Then turn down at a forty-five degree angle and call "IN".

Your target on this first diagonal is just right of center. Concentrate on flying straight and staying on a forty-five degree diagonal. Then, when you have descended half way down the window, push a sharp right turn that angles you back to the left on another forty-five degree dive. Make a mental note of the point in the sky where you made this turn. You're going to do another one here later.

As you approach the ground, get ready for another right turn. Pull-pull to turn up, over, and reverse direction. Pull-right to power in, and pull-left to power out. Your objective is to be flying back to the right in a forty-five degree climb, parallel to the dive you just finished.

PULL-RIGHT TO POWER INTO THE TURN

Don't make this turn too close to the ground. When you complete a "mirror" of it on the opposite side of the window, you will be turning under and will need all the room you can get to avoid hitting bottom.

PULL-LEFT TO POWER OUT AND STRAIGHTEN

Continue your straight diagonal climb all the way to the top of the window. Make your turn there the same size and shape as the one you performed near the ground. This should swing you around on another parallel line. If you took it all the way to the ground, it would exactly overlap the second line of the maneuver. But you're not going to do that. Instead, you're going to do another sharp corner, precisely where you flew the first one a few moments ago.

This is the only left turn in the figure. Push hard to make another clean corner that extends the first line of the maneuver. As you approach the ground, prepare another pull-turn that loops you under and back up to the left on a final forty-five degree climb. Now all you need to do is fly straight and parallel to your first line until you approach the top of the window and call "OUT".

Tubular X is obviously an advanced maneuver with some difficult spacing problems. Remember that all the diagonal lines are flown at a forty-five degree angle, and cross each other at right angles. Dives and climbs are all equal distance apart. To make this work, each of the reverse turns has to be exactly the same size.

Another thing we tried to point out, is that the two corners in the figure are right on top of each other. Fly them so that your dives would overlap if they were extended in the sky. Now go practice!

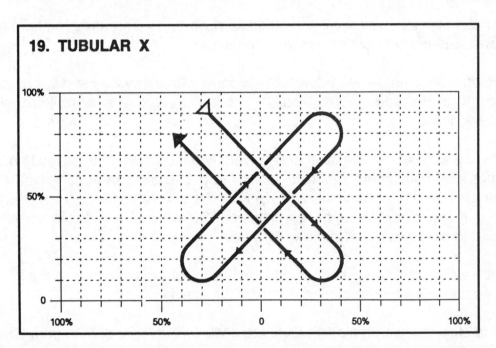

19. TUBULAR X

Competition Spacing: IN is called at the top of a forty-five degree line, twenty-five percent left of center at an altitude of ninety percent. Bottom turns are centered forty percent left and right at an altitude of ten percent.

All parallel lines are eighteen percent wide. Corner turns are at fifty percent altitude and twelve percent right of center. OUT is called forty percent left of center.

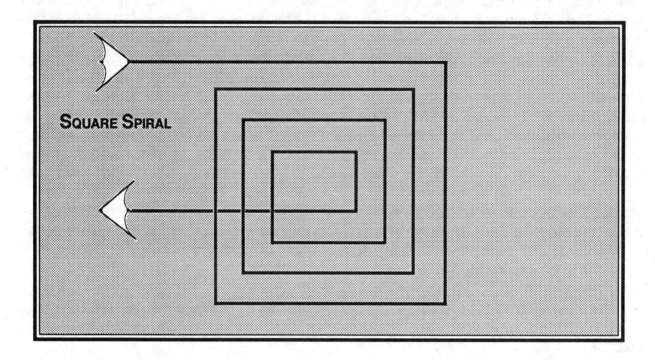

Square Spiral: Let's hope you are in the mood for push-turns. There are fourteen of them in this maneuver, and every single one is flown to the right.

Start in a vertical climb on the left edge of the window. Go all the way to the top and turn in. Stabilize your flight line, and call "IN". Your first job is to fly a long, straight, horizontal line at the top of the window.

As you know, because of the effects of gravity, your kite may have a tendency to drift toward the ground in long horizontals. Maintain a slight "up" pressure by holding your left hand slightly back from the right. Concentrate on flying perfectly parallel to the ground, and set the pace that you intend to hold through the maneuver. You are well outside the power zone, so you may need to step back to maintain your speed.

When you are almost half way out to the right, execute a sharp push turn so the kite snaps a ninety-degree angle toward the ground. Now the fun starts.

Move back to slow the kite in this first dive. Make sure your flight path is perfectly straight, and anticipate the next turn. Time it so you make a sharp right angle just one kite width above the ground.

Move back to maintain speed. Then, as you complete the bottom line, almost half way out to the left, push-left to turn right and start to move back to increase power in the climb.

The maneuver should quickly build up a rhythm now. Notice that the outside perimeter of the figure is a square. This means that each low horizontal pass is going to be just as long as the dive that preceded it.

   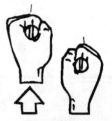

| HOLD EVEN TO
FLY STRAIGHT | PUSH-LEFT TO
TURN RIGHT | HOLD EVEN TO
FLY STRAIGHT | PUSH-LEFT TO
TURN RIGHT |

Each high horizontal is the same length as the corresponding vertical climb. To properly space the boxes, all you need to do is make each vertical climb slightly shorter than the previous one. Move in when you dive, move back when you climb. Focus not only on your spacing, but also on your speed.

It is easy to get confused as the turns come faster and faster. How many have you done? How many left to go??

Try counting the dives to yourself as you fly. Forget about counting corners or any other lines. There are four dives. When you finish the fourth one, push-left to turn right one more time, and fly straight out toward the left edge of the window. If your spacing has been even, this last horizontal should be just below the center of the window. When you pull even with the point where you started, call "OUT". Now go untwist your flying lines.

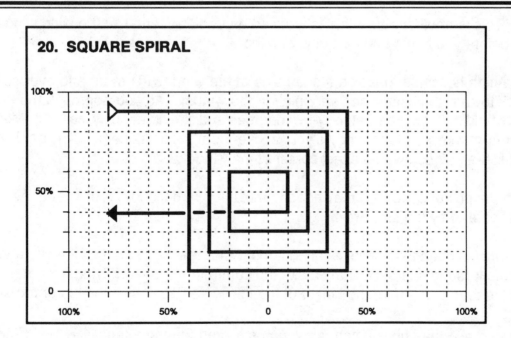

20. SQUARE SPIRAL

Competition Spacing: IN is called eighty percent left of center at an altitude of ninety percent. The first turn is forty percent right of center, the second turn is ten percent off the ground.

Spiraling lines are spaced ten percent apart. Successive vertical dives are at forty, thirty, twenty, and ten percent right of center. Vertical climbs have a length of seventy, fifty, and thirty percent. Each high horizontal is the equal in length to the corresponding vertical climb. Each low horizontal pass is equal in length to the dive that preceded it. The exit horizontal is forty percent above the ground. OUT is called eighty percent left of center.

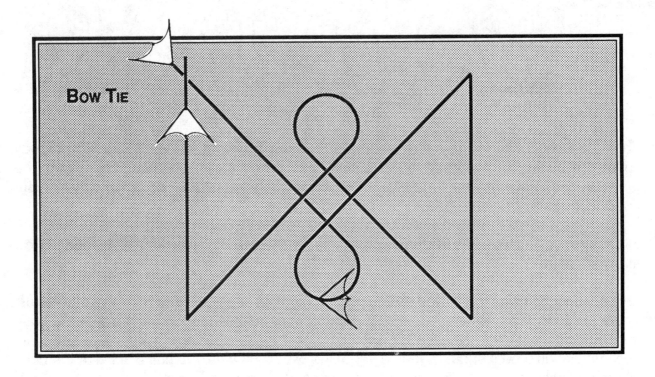

Bow Tie: This is another figure that is focused around the center of the wind window. Find that spot before you begin and fix it in your mind.

Begin in a high horizontal pass on the left side of the window. Turn up and over so you are flying back toward the center and very high in the window. As you approach the point, half way to the middle, angle down at forty-five degrees and simultaneously, call "IN". Make this a short push-turn with your left hand. As you recover from the turn, the nose of your kite should be aimed just a hair below the exact center of the window.

Flying into the power zone, you may need to move forward to slow your speed. As you pass center, prepare to fly the first circle.

Obviously this is not a full "circle" at all, but more of a teardrop. We call it a circle to remind you to make it round, not oval. Don't make the common mistake of flying it too narrow. Also note that the tear is one-third the height of the full figure. Don't fly it too big or too small.

Pull-right to make the curve. Then, as you come around straighten out and aim back toward that spot just below dead center. Remember to anticipate so you don't oversteer. Start releasing from the turn <u>before</u> the nose of your kite is aiming at your target.

ANTICIPATE THE RELEASE
FROM YOUR PULL-TURN.
START A
MICRO-SECOND EARLY.

You should now be on another forty-five degree diagonal line back toward the top of the window, half way out to the right. Move back to maintain speed and get ready for some very sharp turns.

76

When you reach the top of the window, you need to snap around toward the ground. This is a full one-hundred-thirty-five degree turn, so a hard push, or maybe even a combination turn is called for. Anticipate the turn and practice so that the nose of your kite pops right around and flies straight toward the ground.

USE A COMBINATION TURN
FOR THIS SHARP
135 DEGREE ANGLE

Now perform the turn again at the bottom of the window. Do it carefully, because your wingtip will be very close to the ground. Swing around so you are now heading straight toward dead center again.

The second half of the maneuver is a mirror of the first. Concentrate on slowing your flight to keep the turns manageable. Make the angles sharp, the teardrops smooth and round, the lines straight, and your pace consistent. No problem.

Your final vertical climb will be half way out to the left. Fly straight up to the very top of the window and call "OUT".

Flying the Bow Tie may begin to feel familiar after a while. Remember the Mount, which we learned earlier? The Bow Tie is basically two Mounts flown back-to-back. Practice it that way, and it may not seem so intimidating.

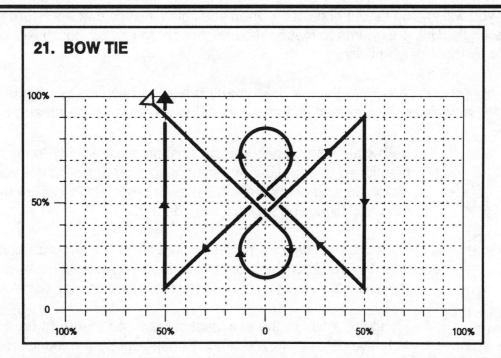

21. BOW TIE

Competition Spacing: IN is called sixty percent to the left at an altitude of one-hundred percent. Diagonal lines are flown at a forty-five degree angle. Teardrops are twenty-five percent wide and thirty percent tall.

Both verticals are fifty percent from center. The upper right turn is at ninety percent altitude. Bottom turns are at ten percent. The first and last lines intersect at ninety percent altitude. OUT is called at one-hundred percent.

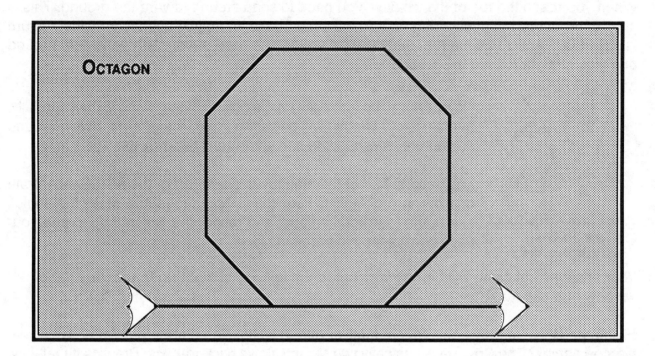

Octagon: This maneuver is not as easy as it looks. Spacing must be exact and each angle precise, or you will end up far out of position when you finish. Notice that each turn is a forty-five degree angle. Use push-turns to make these angles sharp or your figure will look like a rough circle by the time you finish.

Start in a low ground pass from the left. Like many other maneuvers, this figure requires straight flight, very close to the ground. About a third of the way in from the left edge, call "IN".

DON'T LET THE LONG HORIZONTAL DRIFT. PULL BACK SLIGHTLY ON THE LEFT.

Both your starting and ending horizontals are fairly long. As we've mentioned before, your kite may have a tendency to drift toward the ground in long horizontals. Maintain a slight "up" pressure by holding your left hand slightly back from the right.

Concentrate on flying perfectly parallel to the ground, and set the pace that you intend to hold through the maneuver. You are well outside the power zone, so you may need to step back to maintain your speed.

Fly about a fifth of the way past center, and then turn up. Make this forty-five degree angle distinct. Punch your right hand forward so the kite pops. It's better to make the angle more visible than less. Keep moving back to maintain pace, and get ready for another turn.

Now, if you've studied the drawings for this figure closely, you will have noticed something interesting. Diagonal lines are <u>shorter</u> than the verticals and horizontals. In fact, they are nearly ten percent shorter. Use this knowledge to fly the figure perfectly.

The first vertical is not quite half way to the right edge. The next diagonal is almost three-fourths of the way to the top. And the upper horizontal is right at the top of your flying space.

Once you have the rhythm and spacing of the turns figured out, concentrate on flying at a constant speed. Move back in the climbs; move forward in the dives. Both take place well within the power zone. Horizontal lines, on the other hand, are at the very top and bottom of the window, so you will need to move back to maintain speed.

The slower you can fly, the more distinct each angle will appear.

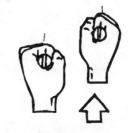

To Keep Each 45 Degree Turn Identical, Push Each One the Same Amount

As you prepare for your final turn, position the kite so the last horizontal line will be exactly on top of the first one you flew when you started the maneuver. Two-thirds of the way out to the right, call "OUT".

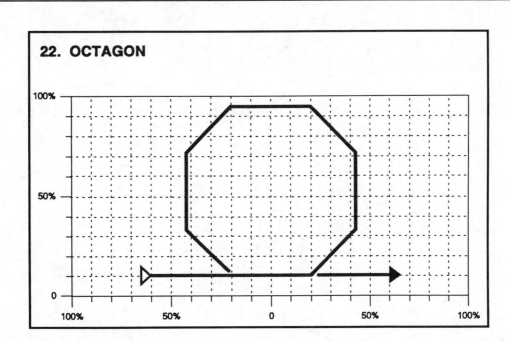

22. OCTAGON

Competition Spacing: IN and OUT are called sixty-five percent from center at an altitude of ten percent. Vertical lines are forty-two percent from center.

The top horizontal begins and ends twenty percent from center at an altitude of ninety-five percent.

Chapter 6: The Magician's Tools: High Performance Tuning

How your kite is tuned determines how it flies. You can leave it set on the "regular performance" marks provided by the factory and probably have no problems. But if you want to fly faster or slower than normal, if you want to adjust responsiveness for fancy tricks, or if you need to modify performance for lighter or heavier winds, then you better learn how to tune.

Sport kite tuning most commonly involves adjusting the bridle lines.

Bridles fulfill three functions on a maneuverable kite. First, they connect the kite to the two flying lines. Those lines, in turn, connect the kite to your handles and then to you. When you pull on a handle, a signal is immediately delivered to the kite at a predetermined point on its frame. Which is a long way of saying that the bridle allows you to control the kite.

The bridle also distributes the force of the wind across a number of points on the kite's frame. When force is evenly distributed, then damage to the kite can be minimized. If the frame is made of fragile lightweight material, or if heavier wind flying is planned, more connection points can be used to further distribute the load.

Finally, the bridle determines whether the kite leans into or away from the wind. In technical terms, this is called the "angle of attack". Because bridles are adjustable, you can change this angle by moving the "tow point" — the place where your flylines connect to the bridle.

So when we talk about bridle tuning, what we are really talking about is shifting the tow point to change the angle of attack.

Most sport kites rely on five bridle points. Lines are tied to the frame at the four joints where the spreaders connect to the leading edge. The fifth point is where the bottom spreader contacts the center spine.

FIVE POINT BRIDLE

**MAIN LINE ON LEADING EDGE
STATIC LINE ON CENTER JOINT**

**MAIN LINE ON BOTTOM SPAR
STATIC LINE ON TOP SPAR**

Usually, one long line runs between two connection points on each side of the sail. We call this the "Main Line". It may go from the bottom to the top leading edge joint, or from the lower leading edge joint to the center spine. Another shorter line connects the remaining bridle point with the Main Line at the tow point. We call this shorter line the "Static Line".

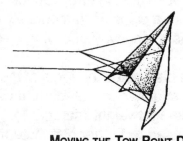

CLIP-TO-LINE ATTACHMENT

LINE-TO-LINE ATTACHMENT

Another thing to notice is how your flying lines are connected to the tow point. Every sport kite you look at will be a little different. Some use clips and swivels, others provide a loop of line that you can larkshead onto.

Go take a quick look at your kite and this will make perfect sense.

Adjusting for Performance

No matter how your bridle is connected to your kite or flying lines, you change the angle of attack by sliding the tow point along the Main Line. Sliding "up" pulls the kite's nose more into the wind. Sliding "down" allows the kite to lean farther back.

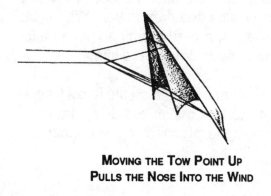

**MOVING THE TOW POINT UP
PULLS THE NOSE INTO THE WIND**

**MOVING THE TOW POINT DOWN
PUSHES THE NOSE AWAY FROM THE WIND**

Tuning is an imperfect science and no one setting is ideal for all flying styles and wind conditions. Experiment. Make small adjustments in the tow point setting, and see how it affects performance.

Try moving the tow point up from the mark set by the factory in increments of about one-eighth inch. Test fly the kite each time to see how it performs. At some point, the kite <u>won't</u> fly. Instead, it will flop over, nose first, when you try to launch. We'll call that point "maximum high".

Now move the tow point below the factory mark. Again, experiment one-eighth inch at a time. Eventually, the kite will be unable to lift off the ground. We'll call that point "maximum low".

Adjustment is a matter of personal taste. Between maximum high and low, the kite will fly. How it flies depends on where, within that range, it is adjusted. Some fliers like tight turns, others enjoy floating around the sky. Most like a mix of both. Unfortunately, no one setting will do everything.

As you experiment, here are some things you should notice:

Leaning the nose of the kite forward by sliding the tow point up will increase the angle of attack. The result will be more speed, reduced pull, the ability to fly farther out from the center of the window, and better control in turns.

Leaning the nose of the kite back by sliding the tow point down will decrease the angle of attack. The result will be more pull, less speed, and tighter turns with a tendency to overspin. Because you now have less lift, you should also find it easier to stall and hover, but more difficult to launch straight or fly far out to the edge of the window.

What this means is that fliers interested in flying fast set their tow point high. Fliers who want more pull with average speed and control use the middle range. And those who want to perfect radical maneuvers and tricks or fly fast, tight turns prefer a lower tow point setting.

Remember that all of these adjustments are <u>small</u> and are made around the mark defined by the kite manufacturer.

Some manufacturers design kites for speed and deliberately set the mark high. Others market kites especially for tricks and set the mark low. So don't be surprised if either maximum high or maximum low is fairly close to the factory mark. The factory mark doesn't really mean anything special. Decide for yourself which position you like and make your own marks.

In simple terms, a quad line kite has eliminated the tow point and extended the bridle right down to your flying handles. Instead of setting just one angle of attack, you can adjust the angle in flight. This, of course, allows you to speed up, slow down, and "fall" backwards. And by manipulating the handles so that the angle on one side of the kite is different from the other, you can do some really interesting turns and loops, too.

Tuning for Wind Changes

The force of the wind on your sail will affect your performance just as much as bridle adjustments will. The kite will move slower and lift less in lighter winds and you'll find it practically impossible to fly at all with a low tow point. In higher winds, your kite may fly too fast to control precisely.

To sustain speed and lift on light wind days, lean the nose of your kite forward by sliding the tow point up.

To reduce speed and power in stronger winds, lean the nose of your kite back by sliding the tow point down.

On particularly high wind days, lean the nose forward to spill wind from the sail and reduce stress on the frame.

With experience, you can use tuning to expand the practical wind range of your kite, or allow consistent performance in a variety of wind conditions.

Many fliers now carry a variety of kites for different wind conditions. Some use completely different makes or sizes. Others prefer a consistent design but use several versions specially modified for high or low wind flying.

High wind kites use heavier sail fabric, reinforced frames and more bridle points to minimize damage. Often, portions of the sail will be replaced with a nylon mesh which allows the wind to pass through. Lighter wind kites replace virtually everything with components that are thinner, lighter, or smaller. They maintain performance while reducing overall weight.

As you might imagine, kites designed for extreme conditions don't perform as well in "normal" winds. So if you choose to invest in a specialized kite, use it for that purpose. Don't frustrate yourself trying to launch a heavy kite in light winds, or risk damage to a lighter kite in moderate breezes.

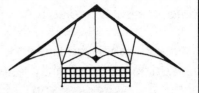

Making Your Own

Taking a perfectly good bridle off your kite and making a new one is a drastic step. But it is an experience you can learn from and you can make a good kite into one better suited to your personal taste.

Regular Bridles: From a structural point of view, long bridle lines are better than short ones. Shorter lines pull the leading edge and center spine together placing tremendous stress on the cross spars. In a stronger wind, the spars are likely to break.

Longer lines cause performance problems. They create drag and turbulence close to the kite, which is the worst possible place. Long bridles also have a tendency to tangle around wingtips during ground moves and trick maneuvers.

Look for a workable compromise.

The recommended size for the long Main Line is the length of your leading edge - the distance from the kites nose to wingtip. The length of the shorter Static Line is sixty percent of the Main Line. Install the new bridle and then test it to mark your preferred tow point positions.

**TOW POINTS
MUST BE BALANCED**

Remember that the marks need to be identically placed on both sides of the kite, or performance will be unbalanced.

Finally, if you plan to be flying in heavier winds and are concerned about damage to your frame, consider adding a second Static Line to help distribute the force of the wind.

Connect it to the leading edge midway between the joints that attach the cross spars. Make this additional line slightly longer so that it hangs slack when not in use. This way, in normal winds, the extra line won't affect maneuverability. But in stronger winds, it will provide the support you need as the leading edge begins to bend.

The Bridle Adjuster: An alternative to shifting your tow point among various marked spots on the bridle line is to add an "adjuster" to the kite's frame.

An adjuster is a short piece of line filled with knots tied at regular intervals. It is attached to the lower part of the leading edge spar where your main bridle line would normally be tied. Then the bridle is connected to one of the knots with a larkshead. You adjust the bridle by shifting from knot to knot.

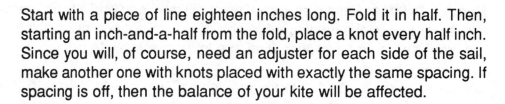

ADJUST BY SHIFTING FROM KNOT TO KNOT

Start with a piece of line eighteen inches long. Fold it in half. Then, starting an inch-and-a-half from the fold, place a knot every half inch. Since you will, of course, need an adjuster for each side of the sail, make another one with knots placed with exactly the same spacing. If spacing is off, then the balance of your kite will be affected.

Now experiment with different knot settings for changes in performance or wind conditions. The adjuster will allow you to return to exactly the same tuning for each knot. Just remember to use the <u>same</u> knot on each side of the kite, and to keep your tow points balanced.

Determine the "maximum high" and "maximum low". Then you can remove any unneeded line from the adjuster.

Constantly pulling at larksheads to tie and untie them can be difficult - especially in colder weather. Try tying a knot in the end of the loop you use for each larkshead. This will give you something easier to pull on and make adjustments a snap.

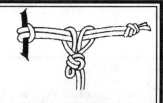

The "Cheater" Bridle: If you are more interested in fast, tight turns than in other tricks, try experimenting with an extra line that connects to the leading edge at the joints where the top cross spar is attached. The rest of your bridle can then larkshead onto this new "cheater" line.

THE ANGLE OF ATTACK INCREASES AS THE KITE TURNS

We call this a "cheater" because it increases your angle of attack <u>as the kite turns</u>. The kite goes faster and pulls harder. Experiment with different line lengths and see how much more you can do.

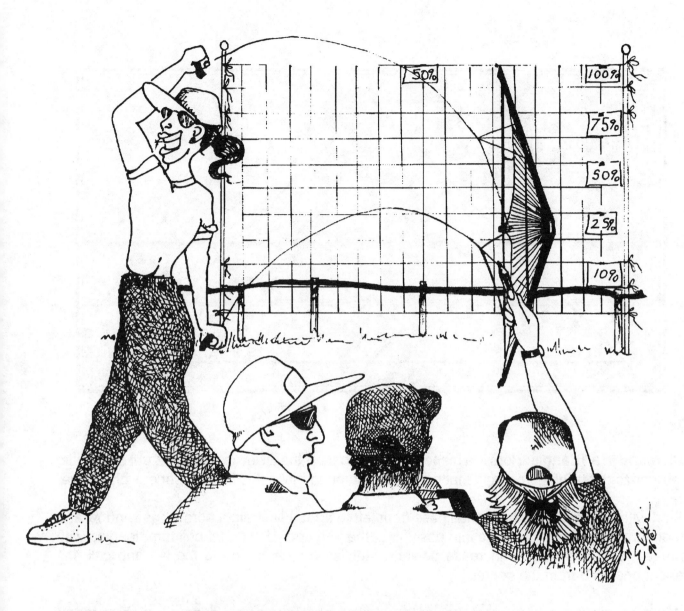

Chapter 7: Most Magical Maneuvers:
Formidable Precision Figures

Here are some figures that are designed to make you sweat. But they are also designed to challenge you and make you feel good about your flying ability. Just remember -- maneuvers with tight angles, multiple turns, and lots of parallel lines aren't more difficult, only more complex.

As maneuvers become more elaborate, it becomes increasingly important to keep the big picture in mind. Focus on details like even speed, crisp corners, and straight lines. But because those details will often come quite quickly, one-after-another, you won't have time to think too much about each of them individually. So think, instead, about how the whole figure will look in the sky. Let your practice, muscle control, and flying instincts take over.

You'll be surprised at how good a flier you are when you stop thinking.

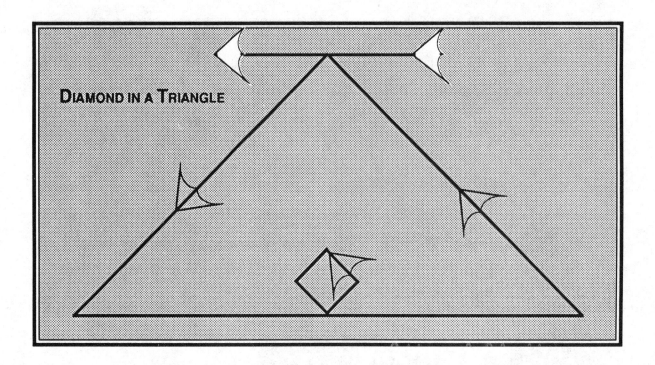

Diamond in a Triangle: Here is a maneuver that is harder than it looks. Long straight diagonals, low horizontals, tight turns, and that nasty little diamond make this figure a serious challenge.

Start with a high altitude horizontal pass from left to right. Fly straight across the window and then turn <u>up</u> and over to move into position at the very top. Use a pull-pull turn, leading with the left, and step back to increase power. Establish a straight line to the left and call "IN" about one-third from the center.

When you reach the center at the top of the window, push a forty-five degree turn. Your target should be the far left bottom corner.

This will be a <u>very</u> long diagonal line and you need to fly it as straight as possible. Any slippage in the angle will throw your proportions off. Any corrections will be very easy for people to see. Remember that you are passing through the power zone and any changes in speed will make your flight look jerky.

USE A PUSH-PULL
COMBINATION TURN FOR A
SHARP 135 DEGREE ANGLE

When you reach the edge of the window, you need to snap around, parallel to the ground. This is a full one-hundred-thirty-five degrees, so push hard. Try using a combination turn to make the angle sharp. Anticipate the turn and practice so that the nose of your kite pops right around and flies back to the right, just above the surface.

At such a low altitude, any drifting will bring you in contact with the ground, so fly straight and careful. Concentrate on flying perfectly parallel to the surface at a constant speed.

You are well outside the power zone now, so you may need to step back to maintain your pace. Set your sights on the center of the window and get ready for the fun part.

Exactly on the center point, you want to angle up at forty-five degrees. It may help to remember that the diamond is centered directly below the entry point of the triangle up there at the top of the window.

Immediately after you turn up from the horizontal line, you need to execute three ninety degree turns. Then finish with another forty-five. Think of it as "push, PUSH, PUSH, PUSH, push". Small pushes for the small angles; bigger pushes for the corners.

The hard part will be recovering on the final turn. The corners will have come so quickly that your reflexes may tend to oversteer and distort the last angle. Your objective will be to finish the diamond and begin another horizontal along the base of the window.

The diamond is designed to be a quarter window tall, but that is still small enough to be troublesome. If you have a choice between flying it larger, or crashing while trying to do it right, fly bigger. You won't lose as many points.

Once you complete the diamond - and you <u>will</u> complete the diamond, fly out to the right edge and snap another tight turn. This will take you back to the top center where you can angle into the final horizontal line. Make this last horizontal an extension of the first one. Avoid the common mistake of turning out too low. Then fly one-third out to the left and call "OUT".

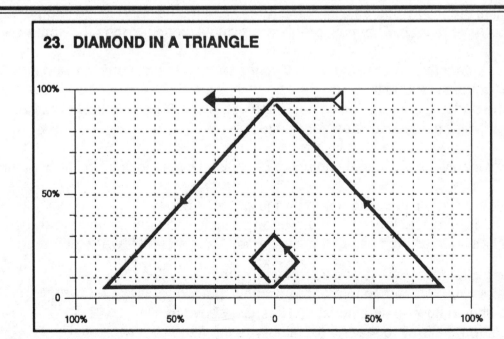

23. DIAMOND IN A TRIANGLE

Competition Spacing: IN and OUT are called at an altitude of ninety-five percent, thirty percent from center. Diagonals are flown at forty-five degree angles. The top of each line is in the center of the window, the bottom is fifteen percent from the outside edge at an altitude of five percent.

The base of the diamond is at the bottom center of the window. It is twenty-five percent tall.

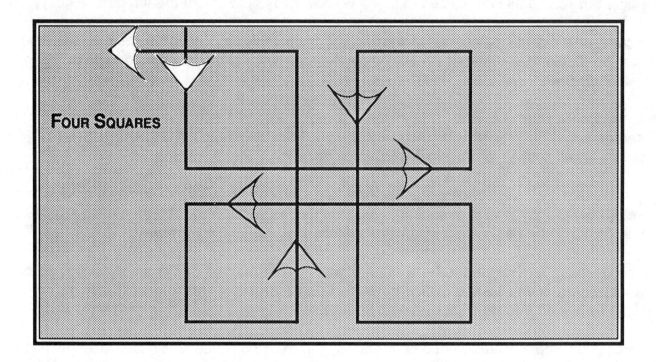

Four Squares: Remember the Dice? This one is even more fun!

Compared to some of the other figures we have been flying lately, Four Squares is fairly easy. All of the angles are ninety degrees, all of the turns are left, and none of the segments are so small that you have to rush. The main problem is flying all four sections the same size.

Try drawing an imaginary cross in the air. Divide the window in half vertically and horizontally. Position your squares around these two imaginary lines. Notice that none of your horizontals extend beyond half way out from the center. Each of the short lines, vertical or horizontal, are equal in length. So are the long lines, for that matter.

So now, we probably have you real confused. Let's see how it looks from the beginning.

Start in a vertical climb midway to the left edge of the window. Move back as you climb to generate extra lift. Then, at the top of the window, turn up and over so you are flying straight down. Call IN as soon as the nose of the kite comes back around toward the ground.

Continue flying straight down. As you approach the imaginary line, halfway between the top and bottom of the window, push-right to turn left. You should now be on a horizontal line just above center that stretches from halfway to the left, to halfway to the right.

PUSH-RIGHT TO TURN LEFT.
MAKE EACH TURN THE SAME.

As you approach the end of that line, push-right to turn up. Angle into another vertical that bisects the right half of the window. Anticipate the turn so you can position it perfectly.

90

Fly straight up to the top of the window, and then turn ninety degrees to the left. Fly straight across the top, and then turn down just before you reach the imaginary line dividing the window vertically in half. These two short lines on the outside of this first small square are the ones that are equal in length.

Now all you need to do is keep repeating the process. Fly a long line to define the inside edges of the squares, two short lines to form the outside edges, and then another long line. "Straight, left, left, left, straight."

Be careful in those long horizontals. As you know, because of the effects of gravity, your kite may have a tendency to drift toward the ground. Concentrate on flying perfectly parallel to the surface, and maintain the pace that you have already set for the maneuver.

At the end of your fourth long line, you should be flying straight up toward the top of the window. Make this vertical the same length as the others, and as you reach the end, turn left. Fly three-fourths of the way out toward the edge and call "OUT".

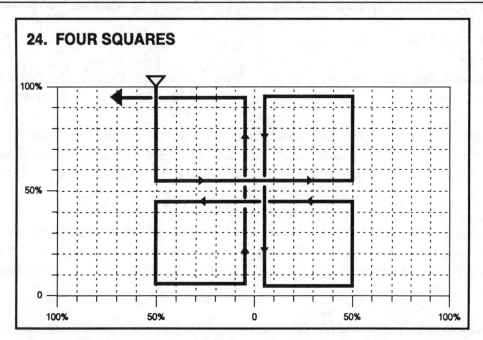

24. FOUR SQUARES

Competition Spacing: *Official rulebook illustrations show the maneuver starting well outside the wind window. Since this is physically impossible, try to fly the figure as close to the illustration as possible.*

Outside verticals are fifty percent left and right of center. Inside verticals are five percent left and right of center.

Bottom and top horizontals are at five and ninety-five percent respectively. Inside horizontals are at forty-two and fifty-three percent.

IN is called at one-hundred-ten percent altitude. OUT is called sixty-five percent from center.

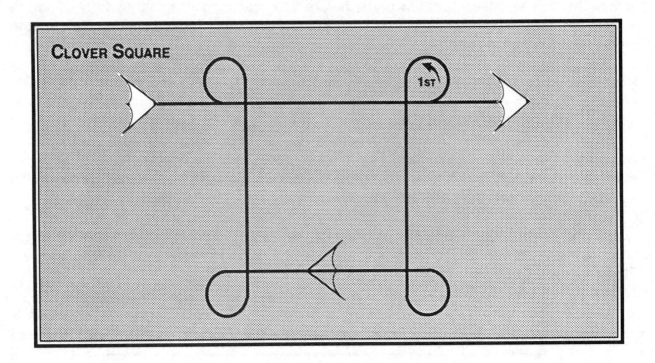

Clover Square: Think of this one as a simple square, centered in the window, but with outside loops at the corners instead of angles. Picture the square, and where the corners will be.

All four sides of the square are equal in length, and the loops should be of identical size. Be particularly careful on the two lower loops. Not only are they dangerously near the ground, but because they both turn under, the inertia of the kite will tend to push it even closer as you turn.

Start in a horizontal pass from the left, about three-fourths up the window. This can easily be reached from a vertical climb on the left edge and a crisp right turn designed to impress the judges before you even begin. Stabilize your straight flight, and call "IN" about two-thirds of the way from center.

Fly all the way across the window. The first loop will be in the upper right corner. Make a mental note of where your horizontal line is, because you will need to duplicate it at the end of the maneuver.

The corner of the square will be a quarter of the distance past center. As you pass the corner, pull back with your left hand and begin a tight, round turn up and over. Pull-left to power in; pull-right to power out. The loop is nearly one-fifth the height of the window, so don't make it too small. But don't make it too big either. Practice so the proportions of the turn match the drawings of the figure.

Each loop is a test of your ability to exit a spin maneuver at exactly the right point. Your goal is to finish the first one and be flying straight down toward the ground. Anticipate, and begin your exit a micro-second early.

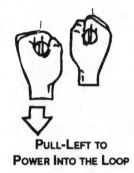

**PULL-LEFT TO
POWER INTO THE LOOP**

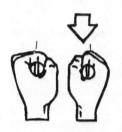

**PULL-RIGHT TO
POWER OUT**

You are right in the power zone now, so you will need to move in to slow the kite's speed. Keep the lines tense enough that you will be able to accelerate into your second loop. Make it exactly the same size as the first one, but use a little more power to avoid any risk of hitting the ground. Time your exit so you are now flying straight across the base of the window, parallel to the ground. The ground pass should be identical in length to the first vertical dive.

Since the bottom left corner of the square is a quarter of the way past center, begin your next turn just beyond that line. Pull-left. Move back to generate more speed and be careful as you turn under and then up. This third loop is the worst one of all.

As you exit the turn, the figure finally begins to get easier. Move back and fly straight up. As you cross what was your first horizontal pass, begin the fourth loop. Again, make it the same size as the previous three. Then fly out to the right, following the path of your original line. Two thirds of the way past center, call "OUT".

Now, take a moment to think about the maneuver you flew, its strengths and weaknesses. Were the sides of the square straight, or did you oversteer to the point where lines between the loops became bowed? Were the loops all identical in size? Were you able to maintain a constant speed through the climbs, dives, and horizontals? Each time you fly a maneuver, think about how you can make it better next time.

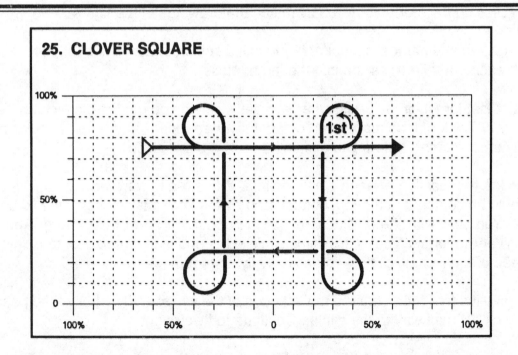

25. CLOVER SQUARE

Competition Spacing; All straight lines are twenty-five percent from the center of the window. Circles are twenty-percent in diameter. IN and OUT are called sixty-five percent from the center at an altitude of seventy-five percent.

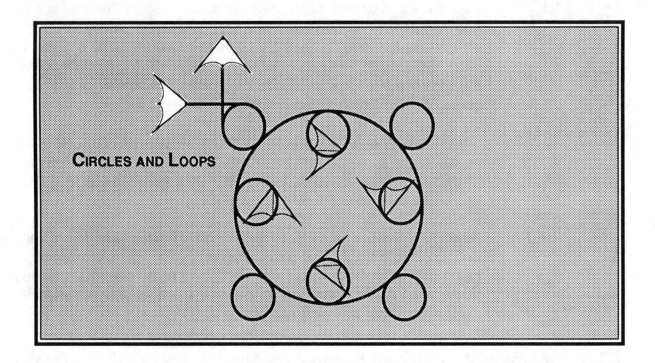

Circles and Loops: Here is another messy maneuver designed to make you dizzy.

Look at the figure closely before you start to practice. Notice that each smaller circle is nearly one-fifth the height of the window. Don't make them too small, but don't make them too big either. Practice so the proportions you fly match the drawings of the figure.

These circles are another test of your ability to exit a spin at exactly the right point. Your goal is to finish each one and transition into the larger circle.

Let's look at that larger circle. Seeing it as a circle will help you get the big picture, but won't help you fly it. Think of it as more of an octagon, with rounded rather than angular corners. You will fly each "corner" before you shift into the next small circle.

Finally, notice the location of each smaller circle. If this really were an octagon, the inside circles would be centered at the top, bottom, and sides. The outside circles would be on the diagonals. You start with the outside circle at the upper left part of the figure. And here is something very important: you fly this same circle at the end of the maneuver too. This means that, instead of eight small circles, you actually fly nine of them.

Ready to give it a try? Start near the top left edge of the window. Fly a horizontal pass to the right, and call "IN" half way to the center. Continue to fly straight.

About one quarter of the way out from center, pull-right to begin your first loop. Concentrate on keeping it round and properly sized. This will actually be a circle-and-a-half, so continue on around past your starting point. Time your exit so you are flying at a forty-five degree angle to the ground.

CURVE SLIGHTLY FOR THE BIG CIRCLE

PULL-LEFT MORE FOR AN INSIDE LOOP

RETURN TO CURVED FLIGHT FOR THE BIG CIRCLE

TRY COMBINATIONS FOR THE OUTSIDE LOOP

Fly the first part of the octagon, curving inward slightly. Then begin the next small circle. This circle is on the inside, so pull-left. Then exit and fly the next curving part of the octagon.

Soon, you should begin to build up a rhythm. Curve for the big circle, turn for the small ones. "Curve, turn; curve, turn." Arc just enough to give shape to the larger circle.

The two outside circles at the bottom of the figure may be troublesome. Power turns close to the ground always involve some risk, so concentrate extra hard to space them right and time your entrance and exit perfectly. Your goal is to make each small circle the same size and position them properly on the larger circle.

The eighth circle is at the top of the maneuver. When you finish, continue around the octagon and prepare to fly a ninth one. This final small circle should be an exact copy of the first one you flew. Go around one-and-a-half times, and exit straight up. Fly to the top of the window and call "OUT".

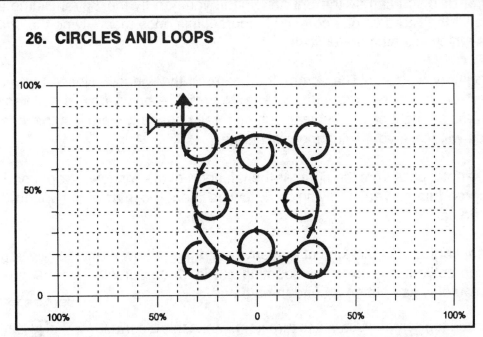

26. CIRCLES AND LOOPS

Competition Spacing: The large circle extends in altitude from twelve to seventy-eight percent. Small circles are eighteen percent in diameter.

IN is called at an altitude of eighty-two percent, fifty-percent left of center. OUT is called thirty-eight percent left of center at an altitude of ninety-five percent.

Competition diagrams are ambiguous as to whether the ninth circle is flown, or if the flier should simply curve around and exit. Clarify this with the judges before you fly.

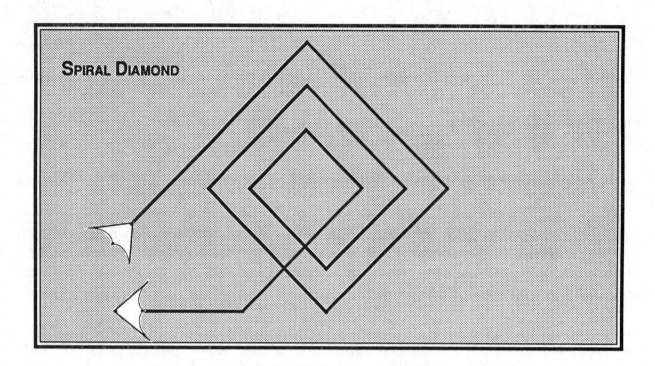

Spiral Diamond: If you can fly the Square Spiral, you can fly the Spiral Diamond. All you need to do is tilt the figure on one corner. Of course, this does mean flying the straight lines as diagonals which is a bit more difficult.

Draw an imaginary horizontal line across the center of the window. Notice that each of the side turns, left and right, are exactly on that line. Now divide the window in half vertically. The two bottom turns are right on this vertical, but the three upper turns are just to the left. Seeing this difference will make your flying more accurate.

Start in a horizontal pass from the right. At the left edge of the window, snap a one-hundred-thirty-five degree turn so you are flying back toward the top center of the window. Stabilize your flight, and call "IN".

It's easy to get confused in this kind of maneuver and forget how many spirals you have left to go. You can solve this problem by counting out loud to yourself. The first line is "one". Remember, you only need to go around three times.

PUSH-LEFT TO TURN RIGHT.

As you approach top center, push-left to turn right. Make this a perfect ninety-degree turn that sends you on a diagonal line to the right. Then, when you reach that imaginary horizontal that divides the window in half, snap another hard angle and turn back to the left.

If you keep focused on those two imaginary lines and concentrate on flying perfect corners and forty-five degree diagonals, the maneuver will practically finish itself.

COUNT YOUR TURNS.
YOU ONLY NEED TO GO
AROUND THREE TIMES

If it helps, you may want to remember that each pair of lines in the top half of the diamond are the same length. Pairs in the bottom half are identical length too, but slightly shorter than the top pairs.

Have you counted off each time you turned up toward the top of the window? If you just said "three", then the turns are coming much faster now. Just stay with your pattern and you will soon be through. Angle back to the right, then down toward the bottom. But on this last line, keep flying diagonally toward the ground. As you near the bottom of the window, about a quarter of the way left of center, push-left one last time. Fly parallel to the ground out toward the left edge. As you pass the half-way point, call "OUT". Relax! It was only eleven turns. The Square Spiral has fourteen!

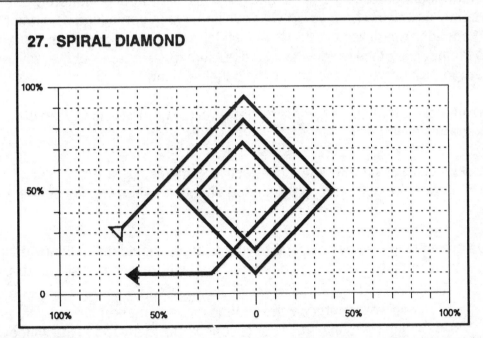

27. SPIRAL DIAMOND

Competition Spacing: *IN is called seventy percent left of center at an altitude of thirty percent. The top three turns are five percent left of center. The two bottom turns are on the centerline. All middle turns are fifty percent above the ground.*

Turns for the first spiral are at ninety-five percent altitude, forty percent right of center, ten percent altitude, and forty percent left of center. OUT is called sixty percent left of center at ten percent altitude.

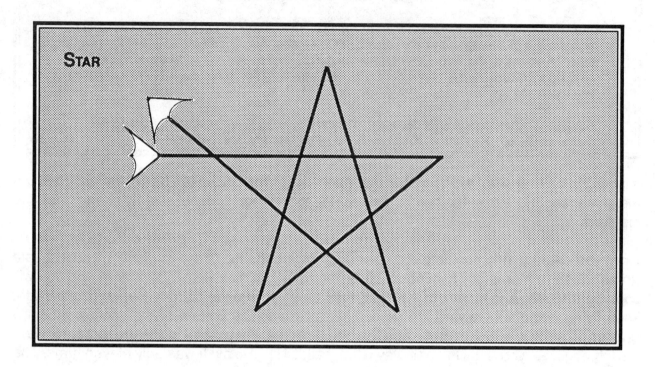

Star:

Star: Before you begin practicing this maneuver, walk out about a hundred feet onto the flying field. Directly downwind from your flying position, place some kind of marker. You can be formal and anchor a small flag out there, or just flop your hat onto the ground. Now, figure out where the boundaries of the window are, and put markers a quarter of the way out in each direction. Then go pick up your handles and let's fly this thing.

Start in a horizontal pass from the left, midway between the ground and the top of the window. Halfway back toward center, call "IN".

Fly straight and level across the window. Fly <u>past</u> your marker on the right side. Then snap the kite around hard. Pivot-right and aim the nose directly at your marker on the left side of the window.

Diagonal dives are nothing new by now, and having a target should make things easier. Move forward to slow your flight, but keep the lines tense enough for another sharp turn.

USE A PUSH-PULL COMBINATION TO PIVOT-RIGHT

As you approach the ground at your marker on the left side, pivot again. Push hard! Your second target is the top of the window straight up above your center marker.

Beginning to get the picture? Approach your mark at the top of the window, pivot, and fly down toward the marker on the right side. Remember, move back when you climb; move forward when you dive. Speed control is just as important in advanced maneuvers as it is in easier ones.

As you approach your right ground anchor, prepare for your last pivot. Anticipate the turn. Make it the same distance off the ground as the one you did on the opposite side of the window.

Turn and fly back up to the left at a forty-five degree angle. This will be a long diagonal, but the hard part is already behind you. Climb out half way to the left edge, and call "OUT".

Using practice markers on the field is a completely legitimate training technique. They are particularly useful in maneuvers that need careful measurements and balance.

Markers aren't allowed in competition, but by then, you'll have practiced enough that you won't need them.

28. STAR

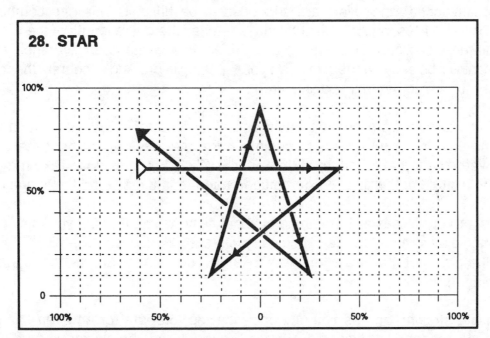

Competition Spacing: *IN is called fifty-five percent left of center at sixty percent altitude. The first horizontal ends forty percent right of center.*

The base of the star is twenty-five percent left and right of center at an altitude of ten percent. The top is at ninety percent altitude.

OUT is called sixty percent left of center at an altitude of seventy-five percent. The final diagonal intersects the first horizontal forty percent left of center.

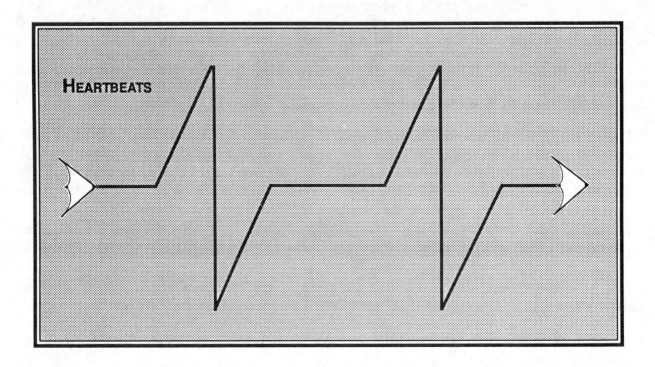

Heartbeats: Advanced maneuvers are supposed to be difficult. This one combines tight turns, lots of parallel lines, and a horizontal that stretches the entire length of the window, but is broken into three sections. This horizontal provides an easy frame of reference for people watching, and it will be easy for them to see if your spacing is off. And of course, the maneuver makes it easy for you to get that spacing wrong.

Start in a horizontal pass from the right that is just below center. Fly out to the left edge, roll up and over, and call "IN". Your goal is to begin a horizontal pass to the right that is exactly halfway between the top and bottom of the window. Fly it nice and slow. Take a moment to memorize the altitude of this line. You're going to need to find it several times again later.

Push-right to turn up. This is a sharp angle of about sixty-five degrees. If you think of a forty-five degree angle as turning "halfway", you can picture a sixty-five as "two-thirds". Or you can just look at the picture. Either way, you need to angle your kite toward the top of the window at a sharp diagonal.

Keep your flight straight, and as you approach the top, prepare for an even sharper turn. Usually, you move back in a climb, but with really sharp turns, the slower you are flying, the easier it will be to get the angle right. So fly slowly. Then, swing the nose of the kite around and fly straight toward the ground. Move in to maintain that slow pace.

At the bottom of the window, prepare for another sharp turn. Push-right to turn left. You want this new diagonal to be perfectly parallel to the last one. If you are flying slowly enough, it will seem like the nose of the kite pivots and the body follows it around.

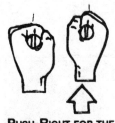   

PUSH-RIGHT FOR THE FIRST 65 DEGREE TURN   **COMBINE A PUSH-PULL TO PIVOT**   **FLY STRAIGHT DOWN**   **THEN PIVOT AGAIN**

Each of the diagonals are fairly short. As you approach the horizontal divider, push-left to resume your pass from left to right and fly over to the right half of the window.

Now, all you have to do is repeat the whole thing again. The challenge in the first half of the maneuver was to keep diagonal lines parallel and angles sharp. You still need to do that in the second half, but now you have the added challenge of positioning the turns at the exact same altitudes as before. Take things slow. Don't let the fact that you are approaching the finish line ruin your concentration.

As you finish the final diagonal, turn once again into your horizontal line. Think of it as one extended pass from left to right with a few bothersome interruptions. Keep flying slow and level. As you approach the right edge, you can call "OUT".

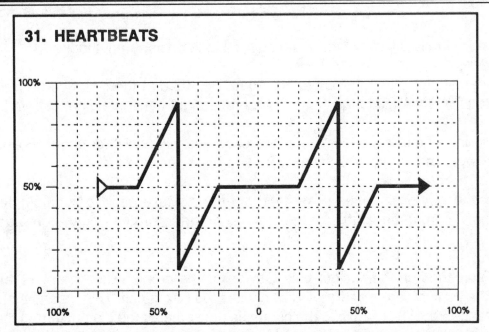

31. HEARTBEATS

Competition Spacing: All horizontal lines are at fifty percent altitude. IN is called eighty percent left of center. The first diagonal begins sixty percent left of center and rises at a sixty-five degree angle. The diagonal line ends forty percent left of center. The second diagonal begins forty percent left of center and ends at twenty percent.

Vertical lines are both forty percent from center. They extend from ten percent to ninety percent altitude.

The third diagonal begins twenty percent right of center. The final diagonal ends sixty percent to the right. OUT is called twenty percent from the right edge.

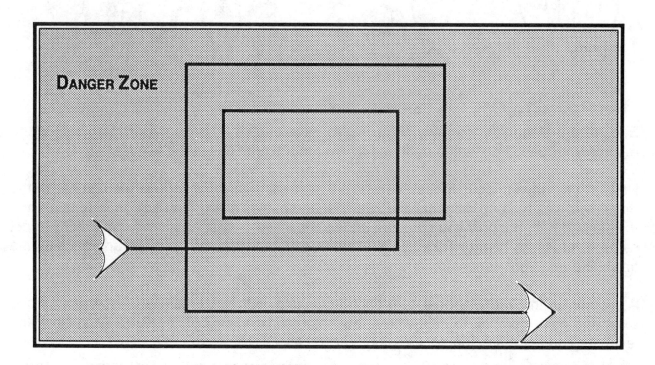

Danger Zone: Finally, we get to do a maneuver that is easier than it looks.

Start in a vertical dive along the left edge. About one-third of the distance from the ground, push-right to turn left. As soon as you establish a straight horizontal line, call "IN".

Use the first line of the maneuver to set the pace you will use throughout. Focus on flying parallel to the ground, and get ready for your first ninety degree turn.

A quarter of the way past center, push-right to turn up. Move back to maintain speed in the vertical climb. Then, three-fourths of the way up from the ground, push-right again and go horizontal.

You're half way through the "inside" box. Obviously, the box is wider than it is tall. But also notice that the vertical center of the window divides the box in half. This means that, as you fly left, the distance from your turn in to the center, is the same as the distance from the center to the next turn down. Prepare yourself, and put that next ninety-degree push in exactly the right place.

The vertical dive will be a short, quick one. Move forward to slow down. Don't make the common mistake of crossing over your first horizontal and flying too low. The turn toward center comes just below the horizontal center of the window.

Push-right again and fly level with the ground. Take your kite out <u>beyond</u> the inside box. Another common mistake is to turn up too soon. As you approach the middle of the right side of the window, turn up and go vertical. Remember to move back as you climb.

Fly up to the top of the window and push-right. There are eight ninety-degree turns in this figure — all of them to the left — and you want to get every one perfect.

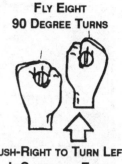

**FLY EIGHT
90 DEGREE TURNS**

**PUSH-RIGHT TO TURN LEFT
IT SHOULD BE EASY
BY NOW**

The upper horizontal line is outside the power zone, so adjust your flight. Don't start to drift down toward the ground before the turn. Fly straight out beyond the left edge of the inside box and then turn into your last dive. Move forward as you fly down.

You are going all the way to the ground here, so as you approach the bottom of the window, add some tension to your flying lines for the last turn. Then push-right one final time.

Don't relax yet. This is a long horizontal line, close to the ground and well outside the power zone. Stop concentrating and you will surely drag a wingtip. Maintain a slight "up" pressure by holding your left hand slightly back from the right.

Concentrate on remaining perfectly straight. Step back to maintain the same pace that you established on your first leg.

When you have flown half way out to the right, then you can call "OUT".

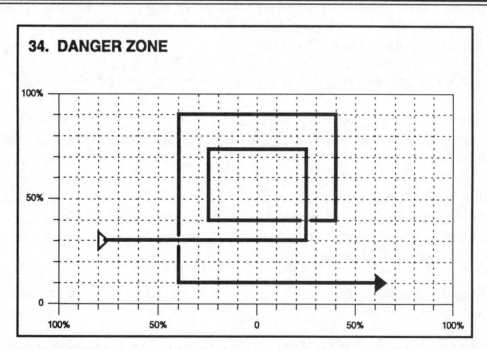

34. DANGER ZONE

Competition Spacing: IN is called eighty percent left of center at an altitude of thirty percent. The first and second verticals are twenty-five percent from center. The third and fourth verticals are forty percent from center.

Horizontal passes are at thirty, seventy-five, forty, and ninety degrees altitude respectively.

OUT is called sixty percent right of center.

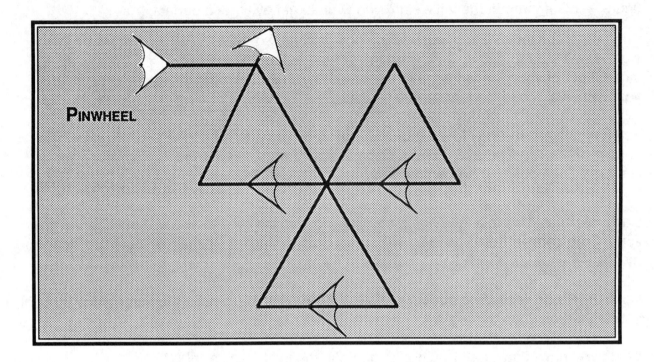

Pinwheel: The first thing you notice about this maneuver are all the angles. Actually, there aren't as many as you think. You can complete the Pinwheel in just five pivot turns, but each of them is a full one-hundred-twenty degrees.

Look closer. What can you see that will help you to fly the figure better?

Notice that all three of the longest lines intersect in the very center of the window. Mark that spot in your mind. This centerpoint is also the middle of each of the lines, so balance the figure around it.

Notice too, that each short line parallels one of the longer lines. And finally, notice that the tops of the two upper triangles are immediately above the outside corners of the lower triangle. And those outside corners are precisely a quarter of the way out from center. These are the kinds of things that judges will be looking for.

Start in a horizontal line from the top left corner of the window. Halfway back toward the center, call "IN".

Now is the time to establish the speed you will use through the entire maneuver. Continue straight and level flying, and when you have come three-fourths of the way back toward center, push-left to angle down at sixty degrees.

Your target on this first diagonal is a spot on the ground, a quarter of the way right of center. Along the way, you will pass though the centerpoint of the window. When you get to the target, push-left to pivot to the right.

Fly parallel to the ground, past center and twenty-five percent of the way out to the left. Then pivot-right again. Your next target is the top of the window, directly above the first pivot point, which of course is twenty-five percent right of center. This will take you through the centerpoint a second time.

When you reach this next target, pivot-right again. Fly downward on a line parallel to your first diagonal. Plan to make your next turn halfway between the ground and the top of the window. Wait for the right moment, and then pivot back to the left in a horizontal pass parallel to the ground.

EACH TURN IS 120 DEGREES

TRY A PUSH-TURN OR A COMBINATION

This long horizontal will take you through the centerpoint a third time. Remember that when you get to the center, you have flown half of the line. Continue an equal distance to the left, and then pivot one final time. The kite should now be on a diagonal line parallel to the sides of the other two triangles. Your target should be the first angle you used to fly into the maneuver. Coincidentally, this intersection should be directly above the left corner of the bottom triangle.

Fly up to the very top of the window and call "OUT". It's easy when you have all these ways to measure!

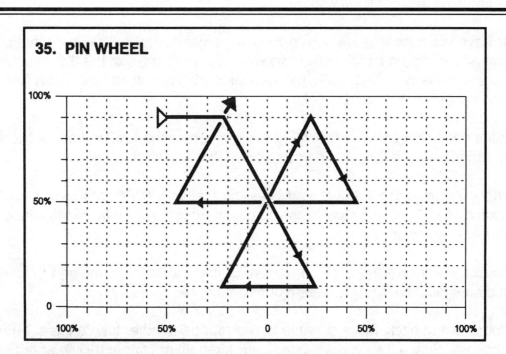

35. PIN WHEEL

Competition Spacing: IN is called fifty percent left of center at an altitude of ninety percent. Upper triangles peak twenty-two percent left and right of center. The base of the upper triangles extends forty-five percent to the left and right.

The base of the bottom triangle is twenty-two percent left and right of center at an altitude of ten percent. OUT is called twenty percent left of center at an altitude of ninety-five percent.

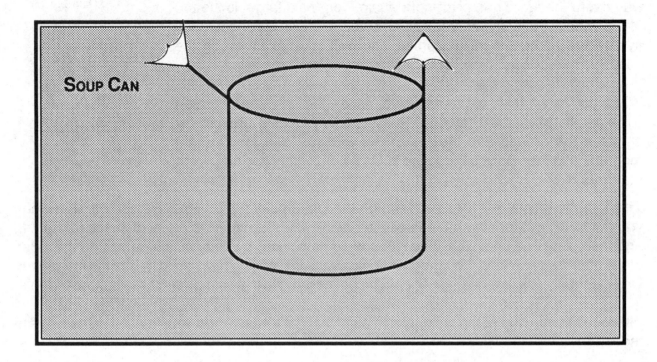

Soup Can: For our final figure, let's try something a little different. Instead of angles or circles, let's combine straight lines with ovals.

What things have you noticed that will help you fly the maneuver better? The overall shape is nearly square and is centered in the wind window. The lower curve of the "lid" exactly mirrors the bottom curve of the can. And finally, the vertical climb that finishes the figure flies straight up toward the right edge of the lid.

Start high on the left side of the window. Fly straight across the top, and about half way out from center, turn down at a forty-five degree angle. Call "IN" right away.

You need to fly a long horizontal oval now. Steer so that your flight path curves slightly and you come exactly parallel to the ground as you pass through the center of the window. Then curve gently back up toward the top.

A common error is to make the oval too narrow so that the figure is tall and thin. The right edge of the oval should be about one-third out from center.

Pull-left to loop up and back. Make sure the turn is rounded, rather than angled. Then fly the top half of the oval. Space it so you will cross over the path of your entry line about one-third left of center. At exactly that point, push-right to angle down. Make this a definite angle that changes you from curved flight to a vertical dive. Now move forward to slow the kite's descent.

As you approach the bottom of the window, prepare another angular turn. Push-right to turn forty-five degrees. Immediately switch to curving flight again.

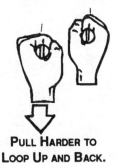

PULL-LEFT SLIGHTLY TO CURVE

PULL HARDER TO LOOP UP AND BACK.

FOR TIGHTER TURNS USE A COMBINATION

PUSH-RIGHT TO ANGLE INTO A VERTICAL LINE

Make the bottom of the maneuver look exactly like the curving line that you used to start the figure. Plan to go horizontal as you cross the center of the window. Be careful not to let the momentum of your flight take you too close to the ground.

One-third right of center, angle straight up. This turning point should be directly below the outside edge on the upper oval.

Now all you need to do is fly straight to the top of the window and call "OUT".

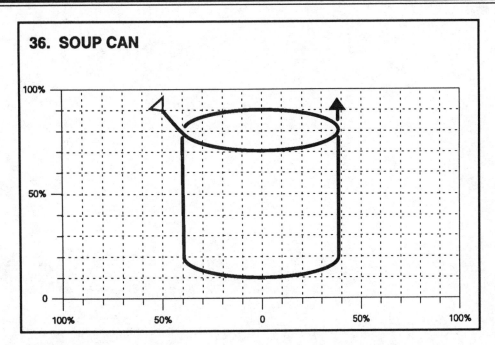

36. SOUP CAN

Competition Spacing: The entire maneuver is centered in the wind window. The left vertical is forty percent left of center. The right vertical is forty percent right of center.

IN is called fifty percent left at an altitude of ninety percent.

The top oval is twenty percent tall and eighty percent wide. It extends from forty percent left, to forty percent right. The highest point of the oval is at ninety percent altitude.

The bottom curve extends from forty percent left, to forty percent right. The lowest point in the curve is at ten percent altitude. OUT is called forty percent right of center at an altitude of ninety percent.

Note that there are minor changes in the spacing of this figure between the Third and Fourth Editions of the International Sport Kite Competition Rules.

The Bee

Chapter 8: Magical Illusions and Hot Tricks

It isn't hard to imagine where some of these "hot" tricks and techniques came from.

A flier jerks on the line to try and relaunch a downed kite. The kite rolls over twice and unexpectedly pops into the air.

A flier accidentally sets their tow point wrong and notices the kite hovers longer.

A flier pushes when they meant to pull and sees the kite flat-spin around.

And then all those fliers and their friends spend weeks trying to analyze and recreate those "accidents" so they can do them again.

If you have been practicing your homework assignments from Chapter 1, you should already have several good tricks in your "repertoire". Sustained stalls, wingtip stands, the leading edge launch, and axles are by no means easy moves. Some of the tricks in this chapter will be easier. Others will be more difficult.

Notice that many of these maneuvers are related to one another. You can start with one basic technique - like a leading edge launch or an axle - and then build derivatives of that move. Adding refinements is how old maneuvers evolve into newer ones.

The point is to build a collection of tricks that will work in a variety of circumstances and wind conditions or transition easily from one to another.

Light Wind Moves

There was a time when fliers cursed light wind days. But ultralight equipment and more efficient designs have left those days long behind.

Fliers now find opportunities in "marginal" winds that allow breathtaking and seemingly impossible moves.

Downward Glide or "Fly Away": In lighter winds, you often need to move back to sustain flight, fly a constant speed, or produce enough power to complete maneuvers. But whether you are on an open field or a marked competition arena, there is a limit to how far you can back-up.

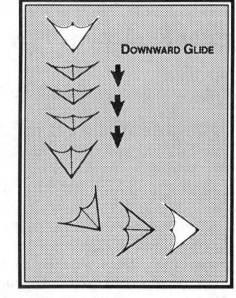

The Glide is one way to recover ground. It lets you gracefully move forward and also provides a good transition to other light wind moves.

Start high in the window. Turn gently into a vertical dive, but instead of tensioning your flying lines and moving back to generate speed, ease tension on the lines and move forward.

If you get it right, the kite will nose away from you and start gliding horizontally downwind. In this position, the kite actually glides faster than the wind is moving. Stay alert and make sure you maintain control.

If you move <u>too slowly</u>, the kite will nose toward the ground and dive more quickly. You won't recover as much ground, and might even crash.

If you move <u>too fast</u>, the kite will flip over on it's back into a stall that is quite difficult to recover from.

Keep just the right tension on the lines and be prepared to run downwind with the kite.

To recover, pull-back on your lines and return to a dive. Make sure you have enough room to turn out before you reach the ground.

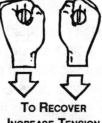

TO GLIDE FORWARD, REDUCE TENSION ON <u>BOTH</u> LINES

TO RECOVER INCREASE TENSION ON BOTH LINES

There are also more dramatic ways to conclude a long fly away glide. You could spin and land. You could plant the nose gently into the ground, and then relaunch. Or you could turn into a 360 as we explain on the next page.

Be creative. If the kite is flying nearly flat and horizontal to the ground, try popping one line in an "axel-like" move to spin it around, nose up.

Float: The Float is similar to the Glide except that instead of flying nose-first, it settles back toward the ground, trailing-edge first.

You can begin a float from almost any point in the window as long as the kite's nose is pointing straight up and the trailing edge is parallel to the ground. Simply move forward and reduce line tension until you stop climbing and actually begin to fall in "reverse".

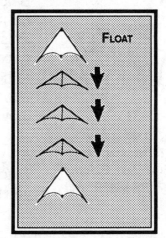

FLOAT

In this case, if you move <u>too slowly</u>, the kite will stop floating and start to climb again.

If you move <u>too fast</u>, the kite will flip over on it's back and stall.

Keep your line tension balanced so the trailing edge remains parallel to the ground. If one wing starts to drop more than the other, increase line tension on that side. Like in the Stall, you are relying on disturbed air flow around your wings to reduce lift. Usually, moving forward smoothly will be enough.

You have already used a Float as part of the sequence in a Three-Point Landing. Try doing a longer one from higher in the air.

Light winds provide a great opportunity to see how well your kite will fly in a direction other than where the nose is pointing. Experiment with transitions. Try an Axle, Float, and another Axle. Or Float to a landing, relaunch to a low altitude, Axle, then Float to another landing. You can try all kinds of moves that involve floating backwards, upside down, or even sideways.

360 Ground Pass: In the Glide and the Float you move forward to reduce line tension and slow the kite's flight. In the 360 and the Up and Over, you do the opposite. You move back to increase speed. The trick is to find somewhere to go.

A 360 is a low ground pass that completely encircles the flier.

Start at the outside right edge of the window, flying back toward center in a horizontal pass about ten feet off the ground. Begin to back up as you pass center in order to generate any extra power that the light breezes may offer. The kite should reach maximum speed as you approach the left side of the window.

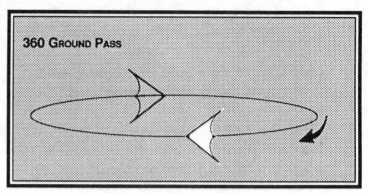

Keep backing up to maintain power. As the kite passes the left edge, you should be backing toward the right side. This will keep the kite moving forward. As it continues to arc upwind, you should begin moving <u>downwind</u>. Keep backing perpendicularly away from the kite.

You will eventually move in a full circle and the kite will follow you on around. The key is to be walking downfield faster than the wind is blowing. This will keep the kite moving upwind. As the kite passes directly upwind, you may find yourself running.

LIKE IN ANY HORIZONTAL PASS, PULL BACK SLIGHTLY ON THE UPPER LINE

Since you are flying from right to left, maintain slightly more tension on the right flying line. Keep the nose of the kite aimed slightly up. This will help maintain momentum and keep you from crashing if your pace slows. Practice flying straight and level in a true horizontal pass, rather than a jerky, uneven line. Of course, the object is to get all the way around - with or without jerks. You can work on perfecting the move later.

As your kite approaches the starting point at the right side of the window, it should start to fly on its own and you can slow down. Or if you like, you can build up some thrust and continue on around again.

Before you start a full field maneuver like this, make sure the <u>entire</u> flying area is clear. Don't just watch the kite as you pull it around, look back every few feet to see where you - and the kite - are going.

Upwind maneuvers like the 360 or the Up and Over depend on you moving smoothly back against the kite to generate "wind".

Remember the effect of line length on the size of wind window. If you are flying on shorter lines, the distance your kite needs to travel to complete a full circle is much smaller. And this means that <u>you</u> don't need to walk - or run - as far either.

Try using less than fifty feet and see how much easier the maneuver becomes.

Up and Over: This maneuver might have been called the 180 Vertical Climb and Dive.

A straight climb usually ends when the kite reaches the top edge of the window and runs out of wind. For the Up and Over, you extend the window by moving back and generating "artificial wind". This, of course, means you have to move faster then the wind is blowing.

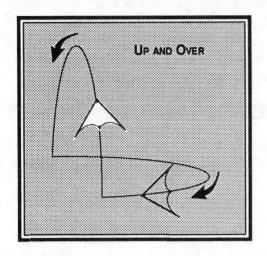

Some fliers like to start downwind, fly to the top of the window, and then run downfield to power over the top. This brings the kite down in a dive on the upwind side of the field where you turn the kite into a 360 and continue running until it returns downwind.

We prefer to start in a 360, using the extra push gained by flying across the window, and fly a horizontal pass to the upwind side of the field. Then power the kite into a climb by running downwind. Even though this is an angle turn, use a pull-pull to add power.

When the kite reaches the top, the wind will be working with you to finish the maneuver. Fly straight down, or shift to a downwind Glide to recover some of that field you have run off.

The Up and Over is impressive, whether you start the vertical turn upwind or down. Try both approaches on very light wind days and see which makes you work harder.

KEEP MOVING BACK

PULL-RIGHT
TO POWER INTO THE TURN

PULL-LEFT
TO POWER OUT

Ground Maneuvers

Just as there was a time when fliers hated light wind days, there was also a time when people thought the only place you could perform was in the sky. Others were intimidated by "ground work". The possibility of damage to the kite, and the likelihood of line tangles or of the kite falling over into an unlaunchable position kept people from trying tricks on the ground.

Times change, and almost every well-rounded routine now includes some kind of ground tricks as well as a landing and relaunch. Back in Chapter One, we walked you through some simple dips and more complicated tip stands. You also perfected the leading edge launch, which is no simple feat. Now, let's try some more low-altitude tricks and techniques.

The Turtle: If you can visualize a turtle on its back, trying to turn over, then you may have some idea what this maneuver involves. It's a quick, eye catching move that involves flipping a grounded kite from a nose down, to a nose up position. Hand positioning and timing are critical.

Start with the kite on a leading edge positioned off-center in the window. The kite's nose should be pointing toward the middle. If you need to, move yourself left or right to shift the kite's relative position in the wind.

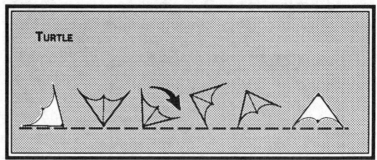

Hand controls and kite movements will, of course, be reversed depending on which half of the window you are using. Let's presume the kite is on the left side of the window. Push with your right hand and simultaneously pull back with the left. The kite will pivot on it's nose and start to swing around.

 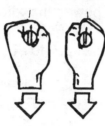  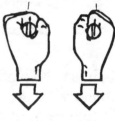

PUSH-RIGHT AND PULL-LEFT TO PIVOT THE LEFT WINGTIP   **STEP BACK TO PIN THE WINGTIP TO THE GROUND**   **PULL-RIGHT TO PIVOT THE RIGHT WINGTIP OVER**   **NOW YOU CAN LAUNCH STRAIGHT UP**

We call it a push to indicate the direction your hands move. Actually, it's more of a "flick". There is no need to be overly forceful.

As the left wing comes forward, <u>step back</u>. This will bring the wingtip in contact with the ground.

With the left wingtip "pinned" to the ground, pull back with your right hand. The right wing will now pivot around. This leaves you in a standard launch position.

It also leaves anyone who blinked wondering what happened and how they missed it.

One of the most difficult aspects of trick flying, is finding good names for new maneuvers. Even worse is getting everyone else to use the same name.

The Turtle is a good example. There are at least two moves people call the "Turtle". One is on the ground, and the other is done in the air. It's understandable that the name is so popular since it is a great description of a move that involves turning the kite right-side up.

Common names and terminology have spread as fliers travel from event to event. The popularity of more timely and global communication, like kite newsgroups on the InterNet, will undoubtedly help encourage consistency.

Or maybe they will just add to the confusion .... :-)

Ground Roll: In many ways, the Ground Roll is similar to the Turtle. You contact the ground, nose down, and leave nose up. But in this case, you rely on the flight momentum of the kite to power a leading edge landing into a leading edge launch.

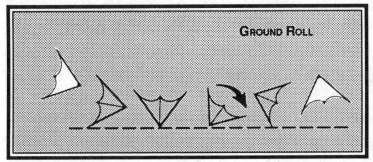

As with most nose-down launches, you will have better luck if you are off-center with the nose pointed toward the outside of the window. Fly toward the ground at about a thirty degree angle.

If you are flying to the right, contact the ground with your right or "lower" wingtip.

As the kite rolls over toward it's nose, push your left hand forward. This is a light, quick jab, not a hard push. Then, as the center spine comes vertical, pull back with <u>both</u> hands. This should lift the nose and drag the left wingtip, similar to a normal leading edge launch.

As the kite comes out of the roll, step back and lift off.

When you set-up for the Turtle or Ground Roll, make sure you are positioned properly in the wind window. The nose of the kite should point toward the <u>outside</u> of the wind.

Wingtip Stab: Here is another "touch and go" move. You touch the ground, and then go right on flying.

Start in a low horizontal pass. If you are flying to the right, push-left and pull-right to turn sharply toward the ground. <u>Immediately</u>, reverse hands. Push-right and pull-left.

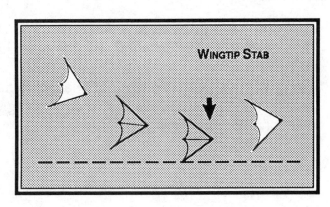

If your hand controls were slower, the kite would turn groundward, make contact on the right wingtip, and then turn back toward the sky. But because you were lightening fast, the kite lurched sideways while still moving down and "stabbed" the wingtip into the ground.

To better anchor the wingtip, step forward and let the kite lean back. Maintain tension on the left line to hold position. When you are ready to launch, pull back with your left hand and turn the kite back into the wind.

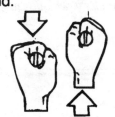

You can use wingtip stabs to vary the pace in a routine or punctuate music. Add several of them to a long sweeping ground pass, or for a real thrill, pop one in at the end of a fast vertical dive.

PUSH-LEFT AND PULL-RIGHT   THEN <u>IMMEDIATELY</u> REVERSE

Wingtip Drag: Instead of sticking a wingtip into the ground, you can try dragging it along. Doing it for a few feet is actually pretty easy. Doing it for a longer distance - now <u>that's</u> hard.

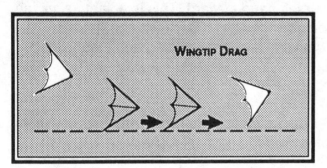

Tip Drags work best when you are steering toward the outside edge of the window. Approach the ground in a low horizontal pass. Continue a smooth descent until your wingtip actually touches the ground.

If you hit too hard, the kite will "nose-in" and you'll end up in a Ground Roll. So maintain steady control.

You want enough downward pressure to keep that wingtip sliding along the ground, and also enough forward motion to keep from crashing. Try moving back to maintain power.

Lock one hand in place to stabilize the line closest to the ground. Then make minor adjustments with the other hand.

A long Wingtip Drag is a thing of beauty. To make it even better, try transitioning in from a vertical dive or finishing the maneuver with an intentional Ground Roll.

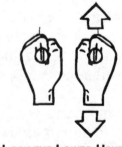

**LOCK THE LOWER HAND
AND STEER WITH THE OTHER**

Slides and Spins

If you can do the Axle, you can do almost anything. Combine the momentum of straight flight with hand movements that stall and spill wind from your sails. Experiment. Practice. Innovate. The combinations of Slides, Stalls, and Spin maneuvers are endless.

Side Slide: This is a move where you use the momentum of a turning kite to push sideways - perpendicular to the normal direction of flight. With practice, you should be able to hold this slide across the entire window.

Start in a horizontal pass to the left. Build up some speed. Then, as you approach the outside edge, use a push-pull to turn under as if you were planning a full loop that would exit in a vertical climb.

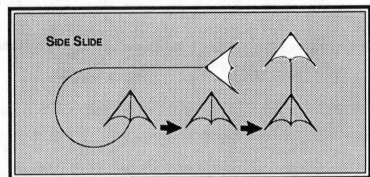

As the spine comes around to vertical, snap your hands back to the normal position and step forward.

Normally, this would stall the kite, but the power of the turn will push it toward the center of the window. Now all you need to do is maintain balance.

Maintain even line tension and keep walking forward, slightly in the direction of the slide. Use a light touch on your handles to monitor line tension and make minor corrections. And remember that setting your tow point low will make it easier to maintain a stall longer.

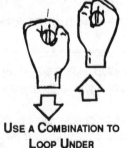

USE A COMBINATION TO LOOP UNDER

SNAP BACK TO NORMAL AND MOVE FORWARD

When you are ready to end the slide, you can pull back on both lines to lift into a vertical, or pull back on one to turn sideways. Better yet, try transitioning into another maneuver - like a spin landing.

Helicopter: This is a tough one. Think of it as a "Falling Axel". A regular Axel is hard enough, but with the Helicopter, you have to worry even more about tangling your lines.

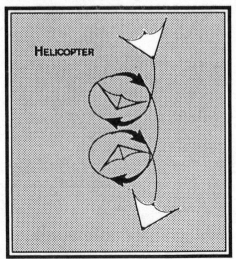

In Chapter 1, you learned the basic steps for an Axel. Push and hold to stall. Pull one hand back to lay the kite on its face. Pop one line to spin. And then pull back on both lines to resume flight.

For the Helicopter, add one more step. Move forward as the kite rotates. Let it float back toward the ground as it continues to flat-spin.

Sounds easy. Right!

Spin Landing: This is a variation on the Three-Point Landing that involves a transition from a spinning turn. Many fliers say it is easier than the more traditional landing since the loop spills a great deal of wind from the kite's sail and it practically lands itself.

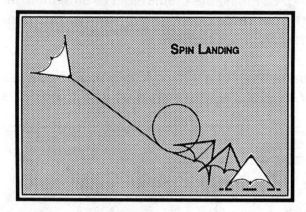

As you approach the landing area, pull the kite into a tight upward loop. Normally, you would pull to power into a turn, and pull again to power out. This time, however, as the kite completes the spin and comes around with its spine perpendicular to the ground, push with <u>both</u> hands. Stall and step forward to drop the kite onto its wingtips.

Hand movements are just like the Side Slide, expect that you step forward more to drop the kite onto the ground.

Landings are usually easier toward the edge of the window, but the Spin Landing can be done almost anywhere. Try adding one at the bottom of a power dive right in the center of the wind. The fast roaring turn followed by a graceful stop surprises people.

You'll find the Spin Landing easier with a turn that goes under, but it also works with a turn that goes over the top. See which one works best for you.

There is more to so-called trick flying than the tricks. Watching one slick move after another gets old. Transitions, variety, and timing are equally important.

The best fliers will combine spectacular trick moves with long, graceful passes and precise turns. They build a sense of drama, and then <u>bam</u>!, explode with an unexpected and seemingly impossible flip.

Plan a total program to get the best results.

Chapter 9: A Smaller Stage: Indoor Flying

There is a breed of fliers who are driven to perform. They experiment. They innovate. They use their imagination to find a way around barriers no matter what conditions, space restrictions, or weather they face.

If the flying space is limited, they use shorter lines. If the weather is wet, they fly under bridges. If there is no wind, they learn to fly without it. And if they have to deal with all three, they move indoors.

Windless indoor flying is the newest sport kite rage. This passion to fly - and to fly <u>anywhere</u> - is largely responsible for the indoor flying movement. With the skills and knowledge you have already developed, you are ready to join the revolution.

Indoor Equipment

There is a difference between an ultra-light kite used outdoors in low-wind situations, and a "feather-weight" kite designed specifically for indoor flying.

Lighter kites can be used, but they won't perform as well. Indoor kites often weigh fifty-percent less and have design features that allow them to hold air longer, float, and glide better than their heavier counterparts.

But indoor kites are also much more fragile.

Sails easily puncture if they collide with solid objects.

Patches and repairs add weight.

Spars and fittings are so thin that they may crack in a crash.

Lightweight lines easily break.

All this means that indoor kites require special care and handling.

Flying lines also require some special considerations.

The maximum length for most indoor applications is between 9 and 15 feet of very lightweight line. This range is obviously governed by the ceiling height, and also by the fact that shorter lines reduce drag and allow more responsive maneuvers. As we explained earlier, light wind maneuvers like the 360 are much easier on shorter lines.

If you are used to flying with handles, consider another alternative. "Feel" is especially critical indoors, and anything that insulates you from your kite may be doing you a disservice. Try keeping a finger or two directly on the lines to monitor any subtle differences in pull.

Tuning

In Chapter 6, you learned the importance of tuning for different flying conditions. Moving the tow-point toward the nose allowed better light wind flying. But at some point, you reached a "maximum high" where the kite tended to overclimb and turn under the wind at the top of the window.

Forget about the wind window. When you are inside with no wind, there is <u>no wind window</u>. You can use the extra lift from tuning "ultra-high" to sustain forward motion. And since there is no wind for you to turn under, you can use the tendency of an over-tuned kite to turn or fly Up and Over maneuvers more easily.

Think of your indoor flying space, not as a window, but as a dome. In this environment, overclimb is good.

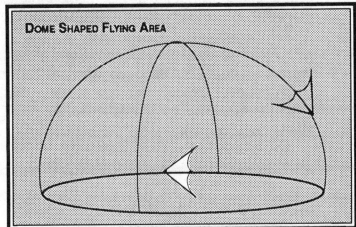

Bridle adjustments of over four inches on your tow points are not unthinkable. Don't be afraid to experiment. If the adjustment doesn't work, just go back to the original setting.

Many of the rules you learned for outdoor flying just don't work indoors. The wind is gone. The window is gone. Hand motions change. Push turns don't work.

If you are ready to fly indoors, be ready to adjust your thinking. Experimentation is very important. Learn new skills that you can take outdoors on the next light wind afternoon.

No Wind Launching

Remember the Pre-launch Checklist?

Safety considerations are paramount for indoor flying. Most of the time you will be moving backwards, so you need to be aware of the boundaries of your space, and of any obstructions it is possible to walk into. If there are other fliers in the area, they are likely to be moving about as well. Decide in advance how to avoid space conflicts and accidents.

Overhead space is also a concern. This isn't simply a matter of banging a fragile kite on the ceiling. Light fixtures are easy to snag and difficult to untangle from. And then, there is the issue of electricity...

Once you have checked your flying space for potential problems, you can begin to plan out your flight program. Lean your kite against a wall or chair in launch position. Then take a moment to mentally prepare your first few moves.

Most fliers find the launch the most difficult part of indoor flying.

For outdoor launches, you normally pull on both lines as you step back to lift the kite into the wind. As the kite begins to pull, you return your hands to the "normal" flying position.

But for indoor flying, the kite isn't going to pull. If you bring your hands back, the only control you will have left is pushing - which doesn't work well inside. Use your feet instead.

Keep your hands slightly extended and move back smoothly to generate lift. For every action, there is an equal and opposite reaction. This means you will need to keep moving to maintain lift. Whichever direction the kite is flying - left, right, and even up and down - you need to exert force in the opposite direction. As soon as you release tension on the flying lines, the kite is going to stall and fall out of the air.

After the stall, you can practice another launch.

Maneuvers Using Motion

There are advantages to flying indoors. You control the wind. You actually generate wind by moving back against the kite. And this means that you decide what happens.

There are three basic maneuvers that provide the foundation of an indoor routine. Fortunately, you learned each of them earlier as light wind tricks. Now you just need to relearn these techniques as no wind tricks.

Try throwing your kite around the room without lines on it. This sounds radical, but is actually a good learning opportunity.

Watch what happens. How does the kite fall? Which way does it tumble? How does it glide?

You can use these observations to extend your flying time, improve maneuvers, or save yourself in an unintended stall.

Indoor 360: The 360 is your basic indoor holding pattern. This is the maneuver you execute maneuvers from, and return to when maneuvers are finished. The only difference between the indoor and outdoor maneuver is that inside, you have no downwind arc in which to relax or build power. You need to keep moving constantly.

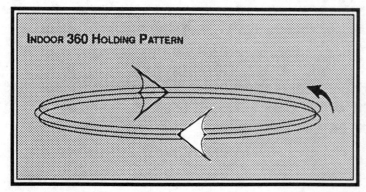

INDOOR 360 HOLDING PATTERN

Start in a horizontal position, and move quickly away from the kite in a circular path. See how quickly you can bring the kite around. As you build confidence and competence, slow your pace until you are walking quite slowly and the kite is hardly moving at all.

Remember to keep the nose of the kite pointed slightly up. This will help maintain lift and keep you from crashing if your pace slows too much. If you begin to get dizzy from constantly walking in circles, try focusing on the kite or reversing direction.

Up and Over: When you move against a kite flying horizontally, you produce a 360. When you move against a kite flying vertically, you produce an Up and Over.

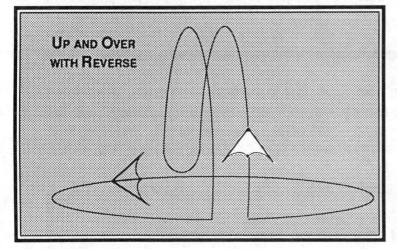

UP AND OVER
WITH REVERSE

Usually, you enter the maneuver from a straight launch, or turn into it from a horizontal pass. Keep moving back through the climb, and as the kite reaches the top of its flying arc, reverse direction and move back against the dive.

Normally, this involves turning around which produces a twist in your flying lines. At the bottom of the dive, you can turn the kite about and begin another climb. By turning the opposite direction, you untwist the line.

Glides, Slides, Stalls and Floats: The Glide and Float are good maneuvers to add to an Up and Over.

In a Glide, the kite lays almost flat in the air, nose away from you. In a Float, the nose points toward you. Give the lines some slack and the kite coasts away. All you need to do is follow it down, maintain balance, and then reassert control at the appropriate time.

To Stall outdoors, you turn the kite so its trailing edge is parallel to the ground, and then push-forward on both lines. But indoors, that doesn't work. There is nothing to "push" against.

Instead, from a vertical climb or a Float, you simply stop moving. The kite will stop too. Then you should immediately resume moving slowly back to hold position.

If instead of moving straight, you move sideways, the kite will edge in the opposite direction. And of course, we call that a side slip or a Slide.

Falling and stalling maneuvers, including the Axel, will be easier indoors. Any hesitation in your backward movement against the kite will have the same results as a push would in the wind. Stopping your movements will drop the kite; slowing will stall it.

Maneuvers Using Turns

The rules for hand movements indoors are almost completely different than for outdoor flying. In the wind, we advise you to keep you arms close together in front of you, never widely spread apart, and never, never over your head.

But consider the indoor Up and Over. As the kite goes over the top, you need to keep pulling against it to generate thrust. You can't move back "through" the floor. So instead, you extend your arms during the climb, and as the kite peaks, you pull them from well over your head back down toward the floor.

This is a good example of the need for big, smooth arm movements in no wind flying.

Turns, on the other hand, need to be as tight as possible. Most indoor fliers prefer larger kites because they provide more sail surface. But kites in this size usually have a width at the trailing edge of over eight feet. If you are flying on lines of less than twenty feet, you have little altitude for the sixteen feet that the kite needs to turn on a wingtip. One alternative is to switch to the smaller sized indoor kites.

Indoor flying has grown in popularity to the point where organized exhibitions or competitions are regularly held. Ballet events with rules similar to outdoor contests are evolving.

To fly indoors for any length of time takes stamina and skill. But sustained flight can be maintained for a surprisingly long time. The current record for uninterrupted and continuous indoor flying by one person is over four hours.

Turns in no wind take practice.

> To compensate for the lack of space, you can use a pull-push, with your hands widely separated, for the tightest possible turn.

> To reverse a horizontal pass, always turn up and over rather than trying to fly under.

> When possible, use a pull-pull technique to power in and out of turns. Step back a little faster to add power.

> Spins are difficult. Flat and falling turns, like the Axel and Helicopter, are easier.

Indoor flying isn't for everyone. It takes a special touch and focused concentration. Some fliers never get it. Others think of little else.

Probably the best part of indoor flying is showing off in front of an unsuspecting audience or just telling your friends what you've been up to.

Kite Flying? In no wind?? That's impossible!

No it isn't. It's just *magic*...

Be Careful Out There...

A common rule book for sport kite competition has now been adopted by the American Kitefliers Association (AKA) for use in the USA, by Stunt Team and Competitive Kiting (STACK) for use in Europe, Australia and New Zealand, and by the All Japan Sport Kite Association (AJSKA) in Japan. Each country hosts a series of events which lead to national titles for individuals and teams. National champions then gather each year for an international competition.

For a copy of the AKA/STACK/AJSKA Rule Book, write to the American Kitefliers Association at 352 Hungerford Drive, Rockville Maryland 20850-4117 USA.

Join the worldwide membership of the
AMERICAN KITEFLIERS ASSOCIATION

◆ Bimonthly Newsletter *Kiting* with Kitevents Calendar, Kite Plans, Chapter Activities, Regional Reports and More ◆ 10% Discount from Member Merchants ◆ $100,000 Liability Insurance Any Time You Fly ◆ Membership Directory and Factbook ◆ Manuals and Informational Publications ◆ $1,000,000 Liability Insurance at Sanctioned Events ◆ Local Club Assistance ◆ Annual Convention, Kite Auction, and Grand National Competition ◆

Membership Application

☐ New Member ☐ I wish to register as a Member Merchant
☐ Renewal ☐ Do not publish my name in the AKA Directory
☐ Reinstatement ☐ Do not distribute my name outside AKA

Name _____ Spouse _____

Address _____

City _____ State _____ Zip _____

Home Phone _____ Work Phone _____

Other Family Members _____

Charge my Visa/MasterCard # _____

Signature _____

My primary interest is: ☐ single line kites ☐ multi-line kites ☐ all kinds of kites

Referred by *D. GOMBERG* My local club _____

3/96 *Kiting*   For info call 800-AKA-2550

Membership Dues	1 yr	2 yr	3 yr	Amount
SPONSOR *Kiting* via 1st class mail includes tax deductible contribution	100	200	300	_____
INDIVIDUAL *Kiting* via 3rd class mail	25	48	71	_____
ADDITIONAL FAMILY per person relatives living in same household	4	8	12	_____
U.S. 1st CLASS MAIL add	8	15	22	_____

International Members please add postage as follows:

	1 yr	2 yr	3 yr	
CANADA or MEXICO	8	15	22	_____
OVERSEAS SURFACE MAIL	10	19	28	_____
OVERSEAS AIR MAIL	25	48	70	_____
TOTAL REMITTANCE				_____

Please remit in U.S. dollars.
Sorry, we cannot take Canadian cheques.

Send this form with your payment to:
American Kitefliers Association
352 Hungerford Drive
Rockville, MD 20850-4117 USA

Cartoons displayed throughout these pages are available as limited edition prints from Kitetoon Originals.

Contact Melinda Ellis at 19040 87th Place SW, Vashon Island, WA 98070, or phone: 206-463-5572.